The Queen
of
Katwe

From One of the Poorest Places on Earth
She Grew to be a Champion

Tim Crothers

ABACUS

First published in the United States in 2012 by Scribner
This paperback edition published in 2015 by Abacus

1 3 5 7 9 10 8 6 4 2

A CIP catalogue record for this book
is available from the British Library.

ISBN 978-0-349-14177-0

Printed and bound in Great Britain by
Clays Ltd, St Ives plc

Papers used by Abacus are from well-managed forests
and other responsible sources.

MIX
Paper from
responsible sources
FSC   FSC® C104740
www.fsc.org

Abacus
An imprint of
Little, Brown Book Group
Carmelite House
50 Victoria Embankment
London EC4Y 0DZ

An Hachette UK Company
www.hachette.co.uk

www.littlebrown.co.uk

To Atticus and Sawyer,
the children of Uganda and beyond

Contents

Prologue

She wins the decisive game, but she has no idea what it means. Nobody has told her what's at stake, so she just plays, like she always does. She has no idea she has qualified to compete at the Olympiad. No idea what the Olympiad is. No idea that her qualifying means that in a few months she will fly to the city of Khanty-Mansiysk in remote central Russia. No idea where Russia even is. When she learns all of this, she asks only one question: "Is it cold there?"

She travels to the Olympiad with nine teammates, all of them a decade older, in their twenties, and even though she has known many of them for a while and journeys by their side for 27 hours across the globe to Siberia, none of her teammates really have any idea where she is from or where she aspires to go, because Phiona Mutesi is from someplace where girls like her don't talk about that.

19th sept. 2010

Dear mum,

I went to the airport. I was very happy to go to the airport. this was only my second time to leave my home. When I riched to the airport I was some how scared because I was going to play the best chess players in the world. So I waved to my friends and my brothers. Some of them cried

1

because they were going to miss me and I had to go. so they wished me agood luck. They told me that they will pray for me. So we board on europlane to go from Uganda to Kenya. The Europlane flew up the sky. I saw clouds looking niece. This time I thought that I was may be in heaven. I asked God to protect me. because who am I to fly to the europlane. so it was Gods power. We riched in kenya very well. I was very tired and they gave me acake it was like abread. I had never tested that before but it was very sweat and I liked it.

When we boad an europlane to Dubai it was very big. So they served us very many eats. I was very hungry. I prayed to God to protect us very well. and he did so. and we riched very well. What I surprised of people which I went with. They were like my parents. they treated me well and my coach treating me as if I was his babby. What I never expected before. That was my first day.

When we riched in Dubai things were different. every was on his own. After then we board the last europlane to take us in Roncha. we prayed so that we rich well. An europlane flew. This time we were along distance from the ground. I think this time I was nearly to tutch on heaven. the clouds were looking niece. then they served me food which I not seen and I was not used to that food. I felt bad. wanted to vomite. So we riched very well. We were welcomed at the airport.

Then they gave us rooms.

The opening ceremony at the 2010 Chess Olympiad takes place in an ice arena. Phiona has never seen ice. There are lasers and woolly mammoths and dancers inside bubbles and people costumed as chess pieces, queens and bishops and pawns, marching around on a giant chessboard atop the ice. Phiona watches it all unfold with her hands cupping her cheeks as if in a wonderland. She asks if this happens every night in this place and she is told, no, that the arena normally serves as a home for hockey, concerts, the circus. Phiona has never heard of any of those things.

She returns to the hotel, which at fifteen floors is by far the tallest building Phiona has ever entered. She rides the elevator with giddy trepidation like it is an amusement park roller coaster. She stares out her hotel room window for a half hour amazed by how tiny people on the ground look from six stories high. Then she takes a long, hot shower, trying her best to wash away her home in the slum.

The following afternoon when she first enters the competition venue, a vast indoor tennis stadium packed with hundreds of shiny new chessboards from baseline to baseline, she immediately notices that at 14 years old she is among the youngest competitors in a tournament that features more than 1,300 players from 141 countries. She is told this is the most accomplished collection of chess talent ever assembled. That makes Phiona nervous. How could she not be? She is playing for her country, Uganda, against other nations, but she isn't playing against kids anymore like she does in Katwe. She is playing against grown women, and as her first game approaches, as she struggles to locate her table because she is still learning to read, she keeps thinking to herself, "Do I belong here?"

Her first opponent is Dina Kagramanov, the Canadian national champion. Kagramanov, born in Baku, Azerbaijan, the hometown of former men's world chess champion Garry Kasparov, learned the game at age six from her grandfather. She is competing in her third Olympiad and at age 24 has been playing elite chess longer than Phiona has been alive. They could hardly be more different, this white woman playing black against this black girl playing white.

Kagramanov preys on Phiona's inexperience by setting a trap during the game's opening and gains a pawn advantage. Phiona sits forward in her chair, leaning over the board aggressively as she often does, with her hands pressed to her forehead, as if she might will her pieces into a better strategic position. Phiona stubbornly tries but fails to recover from her initial mistake. Still, it is the victor who comes away impressed. "She's a sponge," Kagramanov says. "She picks up on whatever information you give her and she uses it against you. Anybody can be taught moves and how to react to those moves, but to reason like she does at her age is a gift that gives her the potential for greatness."

Prologue

21st sept. 2010

Dear mum,

I great you in the might name of Jesus crist. I have written this letter to inform you that this way it was not fine it was raining at morning and it is very cold now. I don't want to eat any thing. Iam not used to eat this type of food. Whenever it riches to break fast I feel like sick and I feel like I want to vomit. But let pray to God may be I will be ok. What I have like from this way they have given us so many gifts even if I have lost the first game but I will wine others I promise you mother. My coach is ecouraging to play very well. But I am sure I will not disapoite him. I am going to work for my best. I will make sure I wine five games even if I am playing strong women. I pray to at God to make my promise possible. In Jesus's name I have preyed amen.

Phiona is lucky to be here. The Ugandan women's team has never participated in a Chess Olympiad before because Uganda could never afford it. But this year the president of FIDE, the world's governing body of chess, has arranged funding for the entire Ugandan team to travel to the Olympiad in the hope of garnering the country's vote in his reelection campaign. Phiona needs breaks like that.

She arrives early for the second day of matches, because she wants to explore. She sees Afghan women dressed in burkas, Indian women in saris, and Bolivian women in ponchos and black bowler hats. She spots a blind chess player and wonders how that is possible. She notices an Iraqi suddenly kneel down and begin praying to someplace called Mecca.

As she walks toward her designated table, Phiona is halted by security and asked to produce her player credential to prove she is actually among the competitors, perhaps because she looks so young, or perhaps because with her short-cropped hair, baggy sweater, and sweatpants, she could be mistaken for a boy.

Before her next game, against Yu-Tong Elaine Lin of Taiwan, Phiona slips off her sneakers. She has never played chess wearing shoes. Lin is stoic, staring only at the board, as if Phiona is not even there. Midway through the game, Phiona commits a tactical error that causes her to lose two pawns. Later, Lin makes a similar blunder, but Phiona does not detect it until it is too late, missing an opportunity that could have turned the game in her favor. From that moment on, Phiona gazes into the distance, hardly able to bear looking at the pieces left on the board, crestfallen as the remainder of the moves play out predictably and she loses a game she knows she should have won.

Phiona leaves the table and runs straight out to the parking lot. Coach Robert has warned her never to go off on her own, but Phiona boards a shuttle bus alone and returns to the hotel, then goes straight to her room and bawls into her pillow like a typical teenager. Later that evening, her coach tries to comfort her, but Phiona is inconsolable. It is the only time chess has ever brought her to tears. In fact, despite the extraordinarily difficult life she has endured, Phiona cannot remember the last time she cried.

Opening

Chapter 1
Land of the Frogs

Hakim Ssewaya, who has lived 40 years in Katwe, stands in front of his shack. The structure fills with raw sewage during the slum's frequent floods.

She had no other choice. Nakito Jamidah had borne four children out of wedlock, including twins who died during childbirth, and she was no longer welcome at her parents' home in the tiny Ugandan village of Namilyango. Jamidah was working as a cook at the same Lugala Primary School where she'd dropped out a decade earlier at age eight, but she still could not afford to support her two surviving children, who lived with their grandparents. The father of Jamidah's children, who maintained relationships with several other women, was a former soldier and a violent drunk who often physically abused Jamidah until she finally left him. Then one day he came to the Lugala School in a drunken rage and kicked a saucepan full of scalding porridge over Jamidah, causing her severe burns. Jamidah feared for her life. She had to go.

So she came to the city.

When Jamidah arrived in Kampala, the sprawling, congested, dusty capital city, in 1971, Uganda was a mess and it was about to get a lot messier. The small East African nation, bordered by Kenya to the east, Sudan to the north, the Democratic Republic of Congo to the west and Tanzania, Rwanda, and Lake Victoria to the south, was nine years removed from its independence from Great Britain, and the former colony was falling victim to the same growing pains as nearly all of its fledgling African brethren. The colonial map of Africa had been drawn haphazardly, as if by children with crayons. Uganda's four primary tribes, who shared no culture, language, or custom, but had previously been bonded by a common colonial enemy, could no longer live in harmony inside the artificial borders. Uganda languished in a constant state of civil war.

The story of postcolonial Ugandan politics is that of a lieutenant who betrays his general. In the same year that Jamidah arrived in Kampala, Idi Amin, the commander of Uganda's army, deposed Uganda's president, Milton Obote, in a coup d'état. Amin would become the most malevolent dictator in African history.

A primary school dropout and former national boxing champion, Amin had joined the colonial army's King's African Rifles in 1946 as an assistant cook before enlisting in the infantry and climbing through the ranks, proving his desire to triumph at any moral cost during brutal military campaigns in Kenya and Somalia. Immediately after the coup d'état, Amin promised free elections. They never occurred. One week after the coup, Amin declared himself his nation's president and eventually bestowed upon himself the title "His Excellency, President for Life, Field Marshal Al Hadji Doctor Idi Amin Dada, VC, DSO, MC, Conqueror of the British Empire in Africa in General and Uganda in Particular." Amin also famously referred to himself as the "Lord of All the Beasts on the Earth and Fishes of the Sea."

Amin was known to order white Ugandans to carry him on a throne and kneel down before him as news photographers captured the scene for the outside world to see. He praised Hitler's treatment of the Jews, threatened war against Israel, insulted other world leaders, and thumbed his nose at Uganda's former colonial overseers by offering to become King of Scotland and lead the Scots to their rightful independence from England. He allied with Libyan dictator Muammar Qaddafi and courted arms from the Soviet Union. Amin ruled through terror, his regime responsible for killing its political and ethnic enemies, both real and imagined, in a horrific slaughter that took the lives of an estimated 500,000 Ugandans. Amin was even rumored to be a cannibal who consumed the organs of his victims.

Amin's eight-year reign would devastate Uganda's economy. In 1972 Amin exiled tens of thousands of immigrant Indian merchants upon which the country's financial infrastructure depended and handed their shops over to his soldiers who sold size 17 shirts for 17 Ugandan shillings because they didn't know any better. Having banished its business class, the country's economy unraveled, leaving half of the population languishing below the international poverty line. Amin nationalized the country's land, evicting Ugandan villagers from their ancestral farms and prompting other tribes to revolt against Amin and his Kakwa tribe. People flooded into Kampala seeking any kind of security. Upon their arrival, many were shooed away to a slum called Katwe where nobody else wanted to be.

Jamidah and two of her sons, Hakim Ssewaya and Moses Sebuwufu (last names in Uganda are drawn from the father's clan), rented a tiny room in Katwe near a petrol station where Jamidah sold alcohol from a stall near the gas pumps. When she began falling behind on the rent and feared eviction, one of her customers told her about an old man down the hill in the swamp who was considering selling inexpensive plots of land. "As much as my mother wanted to come and meet this man," Hakim says, "she was fearing the area because it was wild bush and no one risked going there."

Eventually Jamidah arranged to meet the man, Qasim, instead along Nasser Road, where he was working splicing newspapers into cuttings that were compacted into burlap sacks to form mattresses. Qasim was a Tanzanian who told Jamidah that he'd once worked as a servant for the Kabaka, the king of the region of Buganda and its Baganda tribe, whose ancestral lands comprised Kampala and much of its surrounding area in southern Uganda, and from which the nation takes its name. Qasim explained to Jamidah that he had been working in the Kabaka's palace up high on the hill during the 1960s, when one of the Kabaka's chiefs offered this land to him, thinking it was worthless because any member of the Baganda possessed too much pride to ever sleep in a swamp.

Jamidah agreed to meet with Qasim again, this time on his land, where they surveyed a small spit of dirt, and in 1971 Jamidah became the first person ever to purchase a piece of the Katwe lowlands. She bought her plot for 1.2 cents, but she could only afford a down payment of .8 cents. Jamidah would work for months to pay off the balance.

Katwe was a bush area of about four square kilometers filled with elephant grass, mango trees, yams, and countless frogs. Every evening the frogs bellowed out such a cacophonous din that it was difficult for Hakim and Moses to sleep. Jamidah began referring to the area claimed by Qasim as Nkere, which translates to "land of the frogs," and would eventually be recognized as one of 19 zones that comprise the enormous slum known as Katwe.

Qasim was an eccentric old man who dressed in a ska made of sewn-together socks, stuck coins in his ears, and never wore shoes. His tiny house stood within a thicket of trees and was surrounded by beehives and green snakes. Hakim suspected that Qasim, who claimed to be more than 80 years old, was a witch doctor.

Jamidah's land was only a short distance from Qasim's house, so Qasim would often summon the young Hakim to fetch him fresh water or to help him prepare a freshly butchered cow's head for eating, all the while narrating stories for Hakim about how the Kabaka mobilized his forces for battle with other tribes. Every evening Qasim would build a fire in his small shack and sing songs in a mysterious language that Hakim did not understand.

One day Hakim's mother was suddenly forced to leave her stall at the petrol station because the station was purchased by an Indian immigrant who refused to let a black woman sell there. So Jamidah would instead hide beneath some nearby trees to peddle her alcohol. When Idi Amin banished the Indians from Uganda, that petrol station was handed back over to a black Ugandan, and Jamidah returned to work there again. Her business grew and she was able to upgrade the shack on her small plot to include three tiny rooms. She replaced the roof of papyrus leaves with tin sheets to better keep out the frequent rainstorms. She was even able to afford to send Hakim to St. Peter's Secondary School up the hill in Nsambya, where he played such skillful soccer that he became known as St. Peter's Pelé.

Then in 1980 one of Uganda's civil wars spread into Katwe. Because Katwe is viewed by most Ugandans as a sort of blind spot, the slum became an ideal slaughtering ground. Ugandan troops would randomly kill anyone they so much as suspected might be a rebel. One day the soldiers shot Hakim's grandmother, Mariam Nakiwala, who laid outside the family's shack bleeding to death with Hakim powerless to help her. Hakim huddled inside the shack with his hand over the mouth of his two-year-old nephew, Simon, knowing that if either made a sound they would be killed as witnesses. Hakim and his family eventually fled to another area of Katwe for a year, where they regularly saw people burned alive. Soldiers burned one of Hakim's best friends so severely, all that remained was his leg.

But the most consistent menace in Katwe has always been the water. For his entire life in the slum, Hakim has looked at the sky with apprehension. Because Katwe is a natural swampland and the water table is so high, almost every rain floods the area. Sometimes the floods rise so high that Hakim must flee to his roof and it can be days before he's even able to enter his house to begin bailing out.

Jamidah, who died in 1994, would eventually bear ten children by three different fathers, but only Hakim and Moses survive. Hakim works for a taxi company and remains as desperately poor as the day he first arrived in the slum. His wife left him and their six children a few years ago after a particularly massive flood completely submerged their house for several days, but Hakim stays because it is the only real home he's ever known. "For my future time I really feel so concerned with my family that whenever I try to put my head down to sleep, sleep doesn't come," Hakim says. "I must wear torn shirts to save whatever I can for the family. What challenges me most is that I don't have any program for my children. When I die, I don't know how they will continue. Even the following morning, they will not be able to get sugar."

Hakim Ssewaya believes he is about 48 years old and he has lived in Katwe for four decades. During his first 15 years there he saw ten different transfers of power in Uganda's government. Each time a new leader took over, people from his tribe would stream into Katwe hoping to take advantage of having one of their tribesmen in power. Finally in 1986, in yet another coup, Yoweri Museveni became president and has remained in that position ever since—the people of Uganda hardly satisfied, but having grown weary of rebellion and war as failed change agents.

"When the war ended in 1986, people started running back to Nkere," Hakim says. "Many people had fled the area to someplace else in Katwe because of the war, but the moment they realized that the fighting had stopped, they came back. It seemed like they left as individuals, but they came back as three. You can ask yourself, 'Why would so many people experience this kind of miserable place and not vacate?' Because it is a place full of people with nowhere else to go."

They came. They came. They came.

By the time Qasim died, he had sold off all of his land, tiny parcel by tiny parcel, to hundreds of different owners, until there was hardly space left to bury him. His grave is now a sewer trench.

People from remote villages all over Uganda came to Kampala because they believed that life was better in the city where they had access to electricity and better hospitals and schools. They came because there are only so many times that a family's ancestral land can be deeded to the sons of a new generation before there is no land left to farm, or they came simply because Idi Amin took their land and they were unable to reclaim it. They came because they learned that foreign aid reaches people in the city first and often never makes it to the countryside at all. They came to escape the wars that were usually fought in the bush. They came to find treatment for the AIDS virus that at its zenith had stricken an estimated 15 percent of Uganda's adult population, spread largely through unprotected sex. They came because money didn't exist in the villages and they felt rich somehow if they touched a few shillings every day, even if they earned less than was necessary to survive.

So they came. But then what?

"It is a trap," says John Michael Mugerwa, a Pentecostal bishop and native Ugandan who worked in Katwe for nearly three decades.

"You leave your village with big dreams because you associate every-thing good and nice and successful and prosperous to the city and people will go to any lengths to get there, only to discover it is not as they thought. Money does not grow on trees in Kampala. The trap is that when you leave the village to come to the city, you've made a promise to the people at home that you're going to live a better life. Many times you've sold off everything you own to come, so there is nothing to go back to."

Then what?

"Imagine you literally have no skills except for subsistence agri-culture, tilling the land, sewing seeds, weeding, and you have not been educated or taught other skills that translate to the city," Mugerwa says. "When you arrive in Kampala you almost become a fugitive, not because you've done anything wrong, but because you have nothing to do, so you need to go to a place where you will not be easily detected and you will not fall into the wrong hands of the law. Usually that will push you to a place where life is shadowy, where no one will ask who you are or where you are from or even notice that you exist."

So they came. And they stayed. And they needed a place to get lost. Katwe.

The largest of eight slums in Kampala, Katwe (kot-WAY) is one of the worst places on earth. The slum is often so severely flooded that many residents sleep in hammocks suspended just beneath their roofs to avoid drowning. Raw sewage runs through trenches beside the alley-ways of the slum and floods carry it inside people's shacks. The human waste from neighboring downtown Kampala is also dumped directly into Katwe. There is no sanitation service. Flies are everywhere. The stench is appalling.

When it isn't flooded, Katwe's land is packed dirt, fouled by the sewage. Nothing grows there. Stray dogs and rats and long-horned cattle all compete with humans to survive in a confined space that becomes more overcrowded every day. Homes exist wherever someone can find space to construct a makeshift shack, at least until a developer decides that land might have some value and the area is set afire. People are evicted from their dwellings by way of a controlled burn.

In Katwe they say that "running water" is the water you have to run through the slum to get, either from a dirty community well or a fetid puddle. Electricity is far too expensive for most Katwe residents where it is accessible at all. Landlords show up periodically with a sack full of padlocks and anyone who can't pay the rent is locked out of their home.

Katwe has no street signs. No addresses. It is a maze of rutted alleys and dilapidated shacks. It is a place where time is measured by where your shadow hits the ground. There are no clocks. No calendars. Because it lies just a few degrees from the equator, Katwe has no seasons, which adds to the repetitive, almost listless, nature of daily life. Every day is just like the next. Survival in Katwe depends on courage and determination as well as guile and luck. During Amin's regime when Uganda suffered through a foreign trade embargo, Katwe became known as a mecca for spare parts. Anything that could be sold on the black market could be found in Katwe, where the people developed a vital resourcefulness amid the squalor.

If you live in Katwe, the rest of the Ugandan population would prefer that you stay there. In the more stable neighborhoods that surround Katwe, homes and petrol stations and supermarkets are patrolled by uniformed security guards with AK-47s. The skyscrapers of downtown Kampala are in view from any dwelling in Katwe, just steps away. Children of the slum venture to the city center daily to beg or pickpocket and then commute back to Katwe to sleep at night.

In Katwe, life is so transient that it is often hard to identify which children belong to which adults. It is a population of single mothers and their kids tossed randomly from one shack to another. Everybody is on the move, but nobody ever leaves. It is said that if you are born in Katwe, you die in Katwe. Death from disease or violence or famine or neglect touches everyone in the slum, yet individual tragedies are not dwelled upon because they occur so frequently. Most of the children of Katwe are fatherless and the men in their lives often beat or abuse them. The women of Katwe are valued by men for little more than sex and childcare. Many women in the slum are sex workers who eventually become pregnant, but can't afford to stop working in the trade. They must leave their children locked in the shack at night and it is not uncommon for them to return home in the early morning to find their kids have drowned in a flood or died in a fire after knocking over the kerosene lamp they were using as a night-light.

Bishop Mugerwa estimates that nearly half of all teenage women in Katwe are mothers. Due largely to the lack of access to birth control in Katwe and its neighboring slums, Uganda is now the youngest country in the world with an average age of 14 years. The prodigious birthrate produces legions of young children without an infrastructure strong enough to raise them or educate them. Many become homeless and hopeless, with no sense that if they disappeared they would even be missed. Katwe's youth endure an overwhelming stigma, a sense of defeat, and a resignation that they'll never do any better than anybody else in the slum. Achievement is secondary to survival. "What we have is children raising children," Mugerwa says. "It is known as a poverty chain. The single mother cannot sustain the home. Her children go to the street and have more kids and they don't have the capacity to care for those kids. It is a cycle of misery that is almost impossible to break."

By the time Harriet Nakku came to Katwe in 1980, the muddle of decrepit shacks overstuffed with people stretched as far as the eye could see in every direction.

All of the frogs were gone.

Harriet Nakku was not wanted. Not planned. A mistake, like so many other children in Uganda, if it is even reasonable to call a child born without the use of birth control a mistake. Better to say that Harriet was a child her parents hoped wouldn't be conceived. Her mother, Kevina Nanyanzi, was not married to her father, Livingstone Kigozi, who had several other wives. Nanyanzi used to meet Kigozi secretly. One of those meetings produced Harriet.

Harriet was born in Seeta, her father's village, 15 kilometers outside of Kampala. Harriet believes it was in about 1969. Because she was an illegitimate child, Harriet was born at Nanyanzi's sister's house. Nanyanzi then moved with Harriet to her aunt's home in the nearby village of Nantabulirirwa. Harriet stayed there with her mother until she was about six years old and ready to go to school, and that's when Nanyanzi handed the young girl back over to her father because she could not afford her daughter's school fees.

"I stayed at my father's house with my stepbrothers and stepsisters and my father used to leave us there with the stepmum for several weeks without any support, because he used to support other women of his elsewhere," Harriet says. "My father was a womanizer. He had such a bad character. He could only enjoy himself. Because I was not really part of that family, it was not all that easy, so my father chose to take me to the grandmother."

Harriet stayed with her grandmother, Miriam, until a point when Harriet fell sick. Harriet developed wounds and boils all over her body that Miriam could not afford to treat. So Harriet was sent back to her mother. Nanyanzi had since moved to Katwe, where she worked cooking cassava, a nutrient-rich vegetable that is among Uganda's food staples, and selling it from a stall on the street in the evenings. When Harriet's health improved through medicine from a local free clinic, she began helping her mother boil maize and serve it to customers. Harriet began schooling but was twice forced to leave because her mother could not pay her tuition. Harriet studied only through her second year of primary school before Nanyanzi sent her back to her father in Seeta hoping he could continue to fund Harriet's education. Kigozi did not and Harriet languished in the village for several years. "Right from my childhood I used to not enjoy myself," Harriet says. "I wasn't that kind of person who could go and have fun. I don't remember ever being happy."

When Harriet was about 12 years old, her mother brought her back to Katwe. Harriet began the cycle again, in and out of school, constantly dogged by lack of funds, until she finally dropped out for good during her fourth year of primary school, known in Uganda as P4.

"As a child in school I desired to become a nurse," Harriet says. "I always admired them. The attire they used to put on and the lifestyle they led. I admired all their ways. I was very grieved when I had to drop out. I didn't have any hope of studying after I had become a big lady because I left school from a lower class. It could be embarrassing to study with the young ones."

Harriet dropped out of school before she had learned how to read or even to write her own name.

She returned to her mother's food stall. One of Harriet's regular customers was an older man, Godfrey Buyinza, who lived not far from her stall in Katwe. Buyinza would stop by daily to eat and talk with Harriet, often leaving her a little extra money in the transaction. The gratuity was an enticement, a form of seduction in the slums. Harriet began visiting Buyinza at his workplace and sometimes spending nights with him in the hope of continuing to curry his favor. In Katwe, there is often a fine line between courtship and prostitution.

At that time Buyinza was 37 years old, Harriet 15. Buyinza had a wife from whom he had separated and three children in a nearby village and just enough money to expand his family. In Uganda, men like Buyinza are known as "sugar daddies."

"That man could really be a good friend and I started spending more time with him," Harriet says. "Then I got him. I think it had come to six months when I was seeing him and that's when I got spoiled."

Harriet believes she was 16 when she gave birth to her first child. Her daughter was born around midnight, so Harriet called her Night. It was the time of the Bush War in Uganda, and Buyinza returned to his home village of Buyubu because Katwe was too unstable and men there were regularly abducted and forced to join the fighting. Harriet and Night stayed with Nanyanzi until months later when Nanyanzi spotted Buyinza back in Katwe. "My mother used to ask me, 'Where did the father of your child go?'" Harriet says. "So when the man had come back, my mother chased me away and I had to go and stay with the man."

Buyinza rented a house just outside of Katwe along Salaama Road and the three moved in as a family when Night was about a year old. Buyinza worked as a welder. Harriet found a job at a primary school called New African Child, where she cooked porridge and sold food in the school canteen.

"At first the situation was not very bad; though we were not well off at least we could meet some of the basic requirements to survive," Harriet says. "We lived well in our home and at times he could take me to his home village to visit. He didn't make much trouble because he was not a drug addict, he wasn't smoking or taking alcohol. He was just a soccer fan. By then we were all healthy. To me it was a good life."

Over the next ten years on Salaama Road, Harriet gave birth to three more children: Juliet, Brian, and Phiona. Buyinza proved to be a doting father who would often come home at lunchtime and take his children for a meal followed by a treat of sugarcane from a street vendor. In the evenings the family would sometimes go to the video hall to see a movie or take a walk to watch a neighborhood soccer game.

"One thing I remember about our father is that he loved us very much," Brian says. "At night I used to overhear him talking with our mother about how much he enjoyed his time with us."

Two months after giving birth to their fifth child, Richard, Harriet noticed Buyinza's appearance beginning to change. He was becoming gaunt. He stopped eating. Says Harriet, "I was worried and I asked him, 'Are you sick? Should you go to the hospital?' He wouldn't tell me anything. He said, 'Everything is fine.' But he kept changing for the worse. Then one day he disappeared. I had no idea where he was. He left us with nothing more than the money for one day. I became bitter because he said he wasn't sick, so I thought he'd abandoned us."

Harriet struggled on Salaama Road without her husband. The rent went unpaid and because she had left her job during her pregnancy, Harriet had no income. She was eventually evicted and took the kids to stay at her mother's house. Harriet sold the family's belongings to feed her children.

One day in the spring of 1999, about three months after Buyinza left, Harriet received a visit from one of Buyinza's daughters from his first marriage, who told Harriet that her husband was gravely ill. The daughter said that Buyinza was back in his home village, that Harriet and the children must go there right away, and she gave Harriet some money to transport the family to Buyubu. Everyone was shocked at how quickly Buyinza had deteriorated. He was a living cadaver, unable to speak, only able to weep as he extended a hand to touch the baby, Richard.

"I reached the village and I could not even recognize whether he was my husband because he had grown so thin," Harriet says. "I tried to take care of him, but the situation was hopeless. At that point I realized he had AIDS."

Buyinza had known he was dying of AIDS and could not bear to tell Harriet for fear she'd be worried that she had contracted the disease as well. Four days after his wife and children arrived in Buyubu, Godfrey Buyinza died.

"After the burial, my husband's family told me that I was not in position to look after the children," Harriet says. "Initially I refused, but they convinced me that I should leave the children there for some stability and I would go back to Katwe on my own to make plans for what we can do."

So Harriet returned to Kampala with Richard. She had been back in Katwe for just three weeks when Buyinza's daughter returned again to summon Harriet to Buyubu because her second child, Juliet, had fallen sick. By the time Harriet arrived, Juliet was dead. "Maybe Juliet was shocked by the death of her father because she loved him very much," Harriet says. "It may have been malaria, but I believe she didn't want to go on living without him." Juliet was buried beside her father in the family graveyard in Buyubu.

Harriet collected the rest of her family and brought them back to her mother's shack in the slum. Harriet feared for her life. She believed she too must have AIDS and wondered if she would live long enough to raise her four surviving children. Harriet had even begun to ponder suicide rather than suffer her husband's grisly fate. On the family's first night back together in Katwe, Harriet huddled with Night, Brian, Phiona, and Richard on the dirt floor of her mother's shack. "If I am to die," she whispered to them, "let me die with you, my children."

Chapter 2
Katende

Aidah Namusisi holds the only existing photograph of her daughter Firidah
Nawaguma and grandson Robert Katende *(far left)*. The picture was taken shortly
before Nawaguma's death.

"I have no memory of my father," Katende says. "I am a bastard child. I don't know where I was born or when. My birth was not all that easy. My mom conceived me when she was still in secondary school. The man who is my dad was already married and had a family. I was told later that his wife was very angry. She said, 'If I get to see that kid, I will kill him.'"

Joseph Ssemakula was another sugar daddy. He was in his late 30s as he drove through the village of Kiboga, 125 kilometers north of Kampala, early one morning in 1981 and spotted Firidah Nawaguma walking with some friends down the side of the road toward Bamusuuta Secondary School. Ssemakula was smitten by the 14-year-old Firidah. He stopped his car and offered to give the children a ride to school.

"There was a valley the children used to pass through before going up the hill to school," says Aidah Namusisi, Firidah's mother. "That man would put my daughter in the vehicle to help her go through that valley to reach school. He did that daily. It was a trick. Sometimes I would even be in bed sleeping and he would come and pick her up without me knowing and take her to school and that was the plan he laid."

Before long Joseph Ssemakula was arranging to meet Firidah Nawaguma after school and the young girl became pregnant. Fearing the wrath of her mother, Nawaguma ran away from home and began staying with an older brother.

"I tried to look for her and I could not find where she is and then this son of mine told me she is at his place," Namusisi says. "I continued to let her stay with her brother because I was concerned that she would run away again and she might go somewhere where I don't even know where she is."

So Nawaguma gave birth at her brother's home. She was 15 years old and she had a son. She called him Katende, the name taken from his father's clan. Ssemakula already had a wife and five children in another part of Kiboga and could not bring the boy into his home. So Nawaguma and the baby eventually moved in with Namusisi, but the teenage mother quickly became overwhelmed by the challenge of raising a child. "The moment she stopped breastfeeding him, then she gave him to me," Namusisi says. "She told me, 'Let me give you your grandson and you be with him.'"

Namusisi initially didn't understand why Nawaguma would give up her eight-month-old son, but then she learned that her daughter had met another man with a steady government job who wanted to marry her and help her resume her education, and Nawaguma feared that the man would not accept her baby.

So Katende lived with his grandmother in Kiboga, along with another infant boy, Julius Kiddu, a child that one of Namusisi's sons could not support. The trio lived a simple life. On most days Namusisi would wander deep into the bush, pick bananas, and then sell them in the village market to earn just enough money to feed the two children an evening meal that had to be finished before dark.

Namusisi, who was in her early 60s, had been caring for Katende and Kiddu in Kiboga for only a short time when she first heard gunfire in the distance. Rebel leader Yoweri Museveni and his forces, the National Resistance Army, were engineering an insurgency against Ugandan president Milton Obote, who had returned to power in 1980. The civil war would become known as Uganda's Bush War. The main theater of the war would be a region known as the Luwero Triangle. Kiboga rested smack in the center of that triangle. The menacing gunshots were quickly followed by the arrival of trucks carrying armed soldiers. "The rebels had just conquered our area," Namusisi says. "So we were all terrified. I was shaking. It was a war. I had never seen soldiers. I had these two tiny children. I didn't know where to go. I didn't know what to do with them. I called them to where I was and they sat close to me. I asked them, 'Where can we go and hide?' But they could not even talk because they were very young."

The following day dozens of Ugandan army vehicles full of soldiers began arriving from a nearby district. They came looking for Museveni and parked near Namusisi's home. The soldiers asked her questions and threatened her when she didn't answer, but they were not speaking her language, Luganda. Instead they were speaking Swahili, a language she did not understand.

After some time, Namusisi pointed to her children and then to her garden, pleading to be allowed to pick some vegetables to feed them. As she returned from the garden, a group of rebels entered the village and confronted the government troops. A firefight ensued. "I dropped the food, ran into a neighbor's house, and started praying to God: 'How about my children?'" Namusisi says. "I started crying because I thought those men had killed the children. But I found them alive. Then I told the children, 'Okay, let us sit here. We can die from here together. They will find our bones here.'"

The fighting eventually shifted to another area and a local schoolteacher came to Namusisi's shack imploring her to evacuate, insisting it would not be safe to spend the night in her home. Namusisi picked up a blanket and a saucepan and began walking, holding one child in each arm. She had initially planned to go to the local hospital, but there were government troops there looking for rebel casualties and Namusisi feared they might recognize her, so she kept walking until nightfall when she finally begged to be allowed into a stranger's house. She and the two children stayed there for two weeks before she returned to her shack to find it had been ransacked by Obote's troops. Namusisi began staying in her home again until one day when a Ugandan government soldier knocked on her door demanding that she lead him to a particular neighbor. Namusisi believed she would be killed if she refused. As she slowly walked toward the neighbor's home, soldiers shot at her feet to make her walk faster.

Says Namusisi, "The following morning a relative came and told me, 'You know this place is not really favorable to us. You saw how you were almost dying for nothing? We have to go and join another uncle. I will go first and try to find out where his hideout is and if I find him I will come back for you and we will join him.' He came back later and said, 'Let us go immediately.'"

Namusisi left Kiboga with the two infants, Katende and Kiddu. They encountered roadblocks from both sides of the war, but eventually reached the uncle in rebel territory.

"I had these two little children and we were running with the rebels through the bush," Namusisi says. "I had one piece of clothing that I used to carry with me to help me cover these kids. They would sleep on one portion then I used the other part to cover them up. If it rains, then it just rains on us until it stops raining. We used to look for grass to use for tea leaves and we ate nuts from the bush. The children were too small to know anything. Bullets were going over our heads and all they asked me is, 'Do you have food?'"

Namusisi, Katende, and Kiddu remained in the bush under rebel protection for two years, constantly on the move, flowing with the troop movements.

"We could camp in one area for some time and then the rebels would tell us that government soldiers were coming and the rebels would direct us to hide in another place," Namusisi says. "Sometimes we would go six or seven miles at a time, but I had to run to save our lives. I was always terrified and we used to pray together seriously because I knew we could be dying at any time."

Finally, one day the rebels began shooting their bullets into the sky. When Namusisi asked what was going on, the rebels told her that they had conquered the Luwero Triangle. Government troops had ceded the area and it was safe for her to go home to Kiboga. "When we returned to the village, people greeted us as ghosts," Namusisi says. "It was as if they assumed we were dead."

Whenever war refugees returned to Kiboga, they were told to register with the government in an attempt to determine who was still alive. Firidah Nawaguma, who had been working as a nurse at the hospital in Kiboga, learned that her mother and son had returned. Dressed in her nurse's uniform, she rode a bicycle to meet them at the registrar's office. Initially, Nawaguma pedaled right past Katende, neither recognizing the other. But when Nawaguma spotted her mother, she knew which boy must be her son. Nawaguma sobbed as she ran to Katende, lifted him over her head with joy and hugged him. The young boy had no idea who the woman was until she said, "My son, I thought you were dead."

Holding her son for the first time in almost three years, Nawaguma carried him into the government office to register him. "This is Katende," Nawaguma told the registrar. "Robert Katende."

It was the first time Katende had ever heard his first name.

During the next year, Robert continued to live with his grandmother, rarely seeing his mother, even though she lived fewer than two kilometers away. He was a bastard child and his mother's husband would not permit Robert in his house.

After the war ended, Namusisi resumed selling bananas to earn a meager living. She would sometimes journey to Kampala by truck to sell her fruit to vendors at the outdoor markets in the city. Because she could not afford to send Robert and Julius to school and they would cry if she left them behind alone, Namusisi brought the two kids along. The three of them would ride atop the bananas in the back of the truck and when they needed a bathroom break, Robert would throw a banana over the top of the cab onto the road to signal the driver. Those trips were Robert's first connection to modern life in the city. Says Robert, "I found that you touch a wall and a light goes on. You touch a wall again and a light goes off. I thought, 'Eh, how is this possible?'" Another time during one of Kampala's regular power outages, Robert asked his grandmother, "When the power goes off, why do the cars still work?"

Nawaguma eventually left her husband and their four children and moved to Kampala, to the Nankulabye slum, in search of a better life. She also stopped working as a nurse, hoping to earn more money alongside her mother, shuttling back and forth between Kiboga and the capital city, supplying bananas to the Kampala markets. During one of Robert's trips to Kampala, Nawaguma told Namusisi, "You leave the boy here so he can start studying."

It took Robert some time to adjust to his new life in the city. He had never before worn shoes, but his mother insisted he wear sandals so that he would not cut his feet on the broken glass and other debris that littered the slum. The boy complained bitterly about how the sandals made his feet feel. "This piece between my toes, it pains me," Robert told his mother.

Nawaguma valued education and sent Robert to school, where he began to learn English. Raised speaking only Luganda, the most widely spoken language in Uganda, it took Robert some time to catch up with the other children who had been in school for several years, but before long he started performing at their level. "My mom was proud of me, especially my math," Robert says. "I used to do numbers very well."

During the holidays, Nawaguma would send Robert to Kiboga to deliver goods to his grandmother and other relatives. While in the village, Robert would get a chance to act as a bushman. He was given a small spear and taught how to help with hunting warthogs. "The adults would place us children where they don't want an animal to pass and then tell us to make noise and we'd scare the animal toward where it is silent and where the trap is," Robert says. "They cautioned us if we don't make enough noise, the animal will come and kill us, so we had to ensure that we made enough noise. For us it was fun. It was like a game."

By the time Robert had reached P4 his mother could not afford his school fees. She arranged with a friend who taught at Robert's school to sneak him in through a back door. On Robert's first day of class, this teacher asked Robert to come with him for a math lesson in P5 before he could enroll him in P4. The teacher gave a lesson in long division, but before completing the lesson, he was called away from the room by another teacher. The other children began the exercise, so Robert pulled out his notebook as well, because it was math and he thought he might be able to do it.

When the teacher returned to the classroom nearly an hour later, he sat at his desk and called for the students to bring him their note-books to be marked. Eventually Robert took his work to him. "The teacher said, 'Oh, Robert, I'm sorry, I forgot that you were in class. You have done the work? Let me have a look at it.'"

Robert handed him his book and the teacher was surprised to see that he had solved nine of the ten equations correctly.

"Then the teacher said, 'Okay, everyone open your books and if you failed a number that this kid has got right, I'm going to cane you,'" Robert recalls. "He went to the first desk. 'You failed two numbers, two strokes. You failed five numbers, five strokes. This kid is supposed to be in P4 and you are failing them!' I was ahead of almost the whole class. It made my day unfavorable in the school. Everyone looked at me with a very ugly face and I had no friends."

The teacher then asked Robert if he would like to remain in P5 because that would be more convenient for him. Robert agreed, despite his unpopularity with the other students.

But skipping P4 proved problematic for Robert in subjects other than math. He struggled in science and social studies, mostly because he lacked a firm grasp of the English language, which was used for all of the lessons. "I remember one time we were asked to tell the internal parts of the body and I had never seen these before," Robert says. "I left the whole paper blank and I got caned. On my next test, in social stud-ies, I didn't want to hand in a blank paper, so anything I could think of I wrote in. I didn't understand what the question was asking, but I wrote in: *President Museveni*. For another answer I just wrote in *Kampala*. Whatever I could think of, just to fill in every space."

In P3 Robert had ranked first in his class. In P5 he was struggling near the bottom. By that time his mother had remarried and given birth to another child. Nawaguma and her new husband were selling timber and she was prospering financially. For Robert's P6 year, Nawaguma was planning to send Robert to boarding school because she was not comfortable with him staying at a house filled with her husband's children from a previous marriage.

When Nawaguma and Robert walked together around the slum, she had a difficult time convincing people that she was Robert's mother. They thought she must be his older sister because she was still so young. In time, the two developed a very close relationship. "At first I didn't know what a mother was or what a mother was supposed to do, but whenever we were together I knew it felt so good," Robert says. "We had a connection and I grew a great love for her, because I was having a better life."

A month before the end of his P5 year in 1990, eight-year-old Robert was studying for final exams when his mother began making regular visits to the hospital. She had been sick for several months and had tried various treatments, including local herbs from a witch doctor to combat a potential curse placed on her by the vengeful wife of Robert's father. Doctors at the hospital eventually diagnosed Nawaguma's condition as advanced breast cancer and Robert noticed that one of his mother's breasts was nearly detached from her body. Namusisi came from Kiboga to look after her daughter.

One day after school Robert was playing in the slum while his mother was at the hospital for treatment when a friend came to Robert and told him his mother had died. "All I can remember is I was shocked," Robert says. "I stopped playing and I just ran off crying until I reached home and my grandmother was there and she was also crying. She said, 'Katende, my son, who are you left with?'"

At his mother's funeral in her father's home village of Mubango,

20 kilometers outside of Kampala, Robert slowly approached Nawaguma's casket. "I reached her and it looked like she was just sleeping, so I shook her and tried to wake her up," Robert says. "When she didn't wake up, I cried at the top of my voice. I was in the deepest sorrow. I had a lot running in my mind. I felt like killing myself. When people put my mom in the ground, I knew all was over. I had lost everything I had. When she died, I believed that was the end of me."

Lying in a hospital bed just days before her death, Nawaguma turned to her cousin Jacent with a last request.

"I know I'm going to die," Nawaguma told Jacent. "I have five kids and I've just given birth to a sixth. I know the sixth one will be taken care of by the father. Even the other four, their dad is there. But I'm feeling so bad for my son Robert and I don't know how it will go for him when I die. I request if you do anything, don't allow Robert to go back to my mother in Kiboga. If you allow Robert to go back, he's just going to hunt wild animals."

"That is the sentiment which I think turned my life," Robert says. "Because of that statement, my Auntie Jacent took pity on me."

As Nawaguma's funeral concluded, Jacent had not yet decided what to do, but her late cousin's words kept ringing in her ears. She looked at the boy with no shirt and torn pants and she came to him and said, "Robert, I'm taking you to my place. You come."

Jacent was already caring for 12 children, six of her own and six orphans who lived in a ramshackle bunkhouse in her backyard. She and her husband lived comfortably in a middle-class neighborhood in Kampala. Jacent worked in a bank and her husband had a job with the government. When Robert returned to Jacent's home he walked into a sitting room, sunk down into a comfortable couch with a rug beneath his bare feet and sat mesmerized for two hours by the first color television he had ever seen. When it came time for dinner, he was served a plate of meat and carrots, but because he didn't know what carrots were, he sorted them out. "After dinner I was so sorrowful, and I went out into the yard and cried because I didn't know what was next," Robert says. "Even though the house was nice, I felt very insecure. I don't remember how I stabilized."

For weeks, Robert would ask Jacent questions about why his mother was taken from him. He could not shake the feeling that evil forces were involved. "When she died I was convinced that it was because my dad's wife had gone to a witch doctor to put a curse on her and I felt like at that moment if I had seen that lady I would have killed her, even it meant I would be killed as well," Robert says. "I was ready to go. I couldn't find that lady and I had no way of finding out where she was. I was so small that I don't even know if I could have physically killed her, but my heart was strongly telling me to do it."

In her will, Nawaguma had left behind enough money to support her son through two years of school. Robert returned to P5 to complete his exams, but he couldn't concentrate through his grief. When he received the P5 report form, he was ranked in the 66th position out of 72 students in the class. He told himself, "This can't be."

On the day he received his report, Robert walked two kilometers to the city center. He walked rather than ride a bus so he would have enough money to buy a red pen; Robert was determined to improve his position. The red ink in the pen he bought was a lighter shade than the pen used to write the marks, but Robert went ahead and scribbled over one 6, thus upgrading him from 66th to 6th. Then he folded up his report form and walked home.

Robert had been staying with Aunt Jacent only for about three weeks and was nervous about her reaction to his report form. He placed it on the dining table and promptly left the room. When Jacent looked at the form, she noticed immediately that it had been altered. She confirmed her suspicion by examining the individual course grades and realizing they could not possibly add up. She called Robert into the room and asked, "What happened to your report?"

"What do you mean?" Robert said, growing more anxious.

"What happened to your report?"

"Auntie, I'm sorry, I rubbed my report."

"Tell me why and bring a cane."

Robert first ran to the bunkhouse and picked up his report form for P3. Then he got a cane. He had the stick in one hand and the report in the other. Jacent told Robert she was going to cane him, not because he performed poorly in school, but because he tampered with the form. Robert begged forgiveness, showing Jacent how he had finished first in P3, explaining how he had skipped P4, and reminding her that he had taken his final exams just days after the death of his mother. Jacent took pity on him and put the cane away.

During holidays with no school, Robert and the other orphans would wake up at 4 A.M. to travel to the family's farm to do what is locally known as "the digging." They would work all day in the fields, plowing and tilling with hoes and cutting the grass back with scythes, all the while hoping to avoid encounters with the venomous snakes that populate the Ugandan farmland. They would dig until dusk and then sleep six people in one tiny shack. They would often do this for a week before collecting enough food to carry back home for the rest of the family.

"Katende turned out to be a hard-working, obedient boy," Jacent says. "If you gave him a job, he would never say he was tired like the others. He would always finish his work on time."

Whenever Robert and the other orphans returned from the digging, they were reminded by Jacent's other kids that the orphans were a class below in the house hierarchy. "Instead of saying 'Welcome back,' they would say, 'Have you brought me back some maize?'" Robert says. "Then you go outside and cry and you endure. It would be really hard on you, but you had to swallow it up."

Robert viewed his situation as survival of the fittest. At breakfast, Robert was often served a banana, but the portion never filled his stomach, so one morning he pretended that bananas gave him a stomachache. Aunt Jacent started serving him cornmeal instead, which provided a more filling breakfast.

"It was all about *How do I keep going?*" Robert says. "The first three months I would go in the corner and shed tears. I remember once when my aunt told me to give my clothes to some of the smaller kids because they didn't fit me anymore. Those were the clothes that my mom had bought for me new in the city center and so that was hard on me as a child. I knew those clothes would never be replaced. After that I had only one shirt that I wore every day and I became known as 'the kid in the red shirt.'"

Another orphan, Jacent, who was five years older than Robert, was so favored by Aunt Jacent that she had taken her name. The young Jacent was always abusing Robert. One time when she was preparing the daily tea, Robert found a cockroach in his cup. He knew Jacent had put it there, but he could not report her. He poured out his tea and didn't tell anyone.

"I don't like to remember such times," Robert says. "There were times when I asked myself, 'What will I be?' When you've lost a person you've been depending on entirely and then you are just moved to a different place, a lot of bad things happen when you are where you are not supposed to be. You have to submit to anyone who is in that place and they will never be wrong when you are there. You are always the one to blame. I remember one day someone said, 'There is not enough sugar for all of us and it is because of the new people who have come in. Go away, Robert. You shouldn't be here.' That was hard to hear when I had no place else. Every rebuke made me think, 'Is it because I don't belong here?' That really affected me. I prayed, 'Lord, I pray that I get a better life.'"

Says Aunt Jacent, "When Robert used to quarrel with my children he would tell them, 'Do you think I want to be like this? Do you think I wanted my mother to die?' That showed that he was suffering very much."

Robert sometimes considered surrendering to his pain. "Once I was almost tempted and if I had the money I would have left this life," Robert says. "I felt it was better for me to die than go on. I thought, 'This life is not worth anything to me. My mom is dead and now she is at peace. Why don't I join her?' I knew a way of accessing rat poison, but I could not afford it. I could not afford to die."

This is not who I am.

Robert kept repeating that phrase to himself every time he looked at his rubbed report from P5. He was at a crossroads. He needed a reason to live and it would have to come from within. Fortunately, he possessed the one trait so lacking in the other orphans, the one commodity that nobody, not even his tormentor, Jacent, could take from him. Pride.

It happened in an instant early in his first term of P6 while he was working on a math assignment. Robert worried that he had again fallen behind his schoolmates. On all of his exercises up to that point in P6, he had asked for help from friends, because he was not completely confident in himself.

"But that one I did myself," Robert says. "I thought, 'Let me just do what I know.' I thought I might fail, but it came back with eleven correct out of twelve. It was my comeback. I thought, 'Wow, am I the one who did this?' Now I thought I could do anything. I became even more serious. I started really working hard to reach my potential."

After the first term of P6, Robert ranked 37th in his class. By the end of his P6 year he had improved to third in his class. In P7 there were no grades, but he placed in the highest division of his class.

In 1993, 11-year-old Robert attended his first year of secondary school, S1, at Lubiri Secondary School, part of a class of 240 students. When report forms were distributed at the end of the first term, Robert took a quick peek and saw "1st." In his haste, he misread it as "15th." He was thrilled. He folded up the report and went to play after school with some friends. "At one point somebody said, 'Who was the first?'" Robert recalls. "Nobody knew. So everybody was showing their reports. I gave mine to them and then I continued playing, because I knew I was the fifteenth. One said, 'Hey, you guys. Robert's a thief. He was the first and he's just not telling us!' I said, 'What? No, I was fifteenth.' Then I looked again."

Robert quickly picked up his books and ran all five kilometers back to Aunt Jacent's house. When he got there he announced to everyone, "I was the first!" The other kids looked at his report form and said, "Wow, he was the first?" Some of them warned him that the second term would be much harder and if he did not perform well in that term everybody would assume he had been copying.

"My attitude was that every day I see 240 heads and I think they are all trying to take my spot," Robert says. "I must not rest." Robert finished first in the second term of S1. First in S2. First in S3. First in S4.

He liked being first. Sure. Finishing first in his class felt like winning. He enjoyed the competition, even thrived on it, but Robert viewed academics clinically. He saw it as a means to an end. He earned those marks as much for other people, living and dead, as he did for himself. Math and science gave him satisfaction. They did not give him joy. Only one competition gave him joy. Only one competition helped him stave off his demons. Only one competition helped him truly escape. Only one competition was all for himself.

Soccer.

When Robert Katende ran down the soccer field, he felt as if he were running away from his troubles, leaving them far behind, and when he scored a goal, well, that was his personal bliss. Playing soccer was the only time he completely stopped thinking about the myriad problems in his life. "Growing up, soccer gave me all of my happiest moments," Robert says. "Whenever I was on the soccer field, it was the only time I felt at peace."

Robert had first played the game as a child in Kiboga when he and his grandmother repatriated there after the war. The soccer ball then was made with dried banana leaves bound together with vines. Robert and some friends would build two small piles of bricks or take off their shirts and use them to mark the goals. They had no idea what a real soccer goal looked like. They usually played on a dirt compound in the village pocked with trees in the middle of the field, which acted as extra defenders. When it came time to pick teams, Robert's friends always wanted to play on his side.

"I was very tiny and at first I always used my right leg to kick," Robert says. "I had a close friend and I admired him because he could kick with either leg. I used to try to imitate this guy and I kicked with my left leg and fell down badly and I believed the leg could never learn to kick that ball. Then one time I was playing and I hit a ball with my left leg and I scored and that was the end of my game. I ran right home to tell my grandma that I had scored with my left leg."

When Robert came to Kampala, his soccer balls became pint-size milk cartons softened by hot water that would be blown up and supported by rubber bands. Whenever that "pinter ball" struck the barbed wire that lined the schoolyard it popped and the game was over. Robert carried a small pinter ball in his rucksack and he and his schoolmates used to play during every break and every lunchtime. By the time Robert reached S5 he had a reputation as one of the best players in the school. Robert's friends told the school's games master about him, but when the games master came to recruit Robert for the school team, Robert declined because he had no soccer shoes and he had never played with a real soccer ball. He was afraid that kicking a real ball would hurt his bare feet. He also feared playing against much older and bigger boys. But when the games master caned him, Robert changed his mind.

In his very first intramural game, Robert, the only player on the field playing in bare feet, scored the only goal in a 1-0 victory for his team. "I became a celebrity in the school," Robert says. "I was a hero. Everyone at school assembly sang my name in praise."

A prolific scorer, Robert humbly explained to his teammates, "There are two goals on the field. I will handle the offense. You all handle the defense."

Robert scored as many as six goals in one match. He would even take requests to score goals. "If three kids in school would ask me to score a goal, I would score one for each of them," Robert says. "Sometimes I would score and then run to the side of the field to the person who requested a goal and say to them 'That is your goal.' Another time the school offered a full crate of soda if I scored, so I scored and shared the crate of twenty-four sodas with my whole team."

Robert's favorite move was to balance the ball on the toes of his bare foot, flip it over the head of an unsuspecting defender, and then break in alone on the goalkeeper. One day he arrived in class to see that one of his schoolmates had drawn a picture of him on the blackboard. In place of his right foot, a spoon was drawn. So Robert's nickname became *kajiiko*, "the spoon."

His skill became so well-known around Kampala that when Lubiri didn't have a game scheduled, he would sometimes play for other secondary schools on a mercenary basis. The other school would pay Robert a few shillings plus transport, and when he arrived the coach would pluck a uniform off of another player and give it to Robert, and he would usually lead that team to victory.

"Robert was a talented young player," says Barnabas Mwesiga, Uganda's former national team coach. "He had some speed. He had good shots. He could dribble. Those are the three attributes that make a good striker. According to our standards, he had the skill at that time to someday make our national team."

At one point, Robert was invited to a training camp for Uganda's Under-15 national team, but he couldn't attend because it was during the holidays and Aunt Jacent insisted that he do the digging. "At home there was no soccer allowed," Robert says. "They had no idea I was a good player. My Aunt Jacent did not approve of sports. For sure, when I was on the soccer field, I felt like I could do anything I wanted with the ball. If I had more support, I believe I could have played professionally."

Robert watched the World Cup every four years and Uganda TV's taped broadcasts of Bundesliga games from Germany on Saturdays with Aunt Jacent's husband, Amir, studying the moves of players like Jürgen Klinsmann and Rudi Völler.

"I used to have this vision where I could see myself walking up from a valley to a beautiful green soccer field like you just see in a dream and they are playing very well and I remember I could join other people and we would play very serious games and I was making goals. I always wondered where this field was, but I definitely know it was not in Uganda because we don't have fields like that. I looked forward for that always and I knew maybe it would happen."

Soccer allowed Robert to dream. It gave him joy. It became his identity.

"I remember one time after a soccer game I thought, 'If I had killed myself I would not have experienced the fun of scoring those goals. I think it was wise not to do what I was planning.'"

Soccer gave him life. Then soccer nearly took it away.

Moments before the game began, Robert walked over to his friend Allan Sayire and asked, "How many goals can I score for you?"

"If you score one goal," Sayire said, "that will be a blessing."

A 15-year-old three weeks into his first term of S5, Robert was his school's star striker. Early in an intramural game at Lubiri, Robert received a pass along the right wing. He spooned the ball over his defender at the edge of the goalkeeper's box and then sprinted to reach the ball before the goalie. The ball took one big bounce into the air. Robert leaped as high as he could. The goalkeeper lunged at the ball. Robert headed the ball over the goalkeeper's outstretched hands, just as the keeper attempted to punch the ball to safety. The goalkeeper's punch caught Robert's jaw instead, flipping Robert upside down. Robert landed on his head. He doesn't remember anything after that.

The ball trickled into the vacated goal and Robert's schoolmates stormed the field as they often did after goals to congratulate the scorer. But when they reached Robert still prone on the ground, they noticed blood on his face and backed off anxiously. Robert appeared to be unconscious, but his legs were still kicking in spasms. Robert's schoolmates feared that he was taking his last breaths.

The school van was quickly summoned and Robert was driven to nearby Rubaga Hospital. Doctors there were ill-equipped for the severity of Robert's injury, so they ordered that Robert be taken to Mulago, the government hospital. Robert's condition was so grave that they didn't even take the time to transfer him to an ambulance. The school van careened through the congested streets, barreling straight over roundabouts, the driver madly honking his way through Kampala's crawling traffic. By the time Robert arrived at Mulago, he had lapsed into a coma. The doctors did whatever they could to help keep him alive.

Before that school year began, Robert had been forced to leave Aunt Jacent's home because she had retired from her job and could no longer support the orphans. Robert had moved back in with his grandmother, who had relocated to Kampala's Kasubi slum upon hearing rumors of another rebel insurgency in Kiboga. On the day of the soccer accident, Namusisi waited for Robert at home, but he never returned. Mulago had called Aunt Jacent instead, but she refused to come to the hospital, scared of what she might find there. "I feared to go because they said he was not going to live," Jacent says. "I told them to go to the other cousin of mine and let her look after him, because I had told Robert to stop playing sports and now you see what has happened."

Robert's Aunt Dez received a call from Mulago Hospital at around 8 P.M. "I will never forget that call," Aunt Dez says. "They told me, 'Your son has been in an accident. Come to the hospital right away. You are likely to find him dead.'"

Aunt Dez rushed to Mulago and found Robert in a critical state. She spent the night standing vigil at Robert's bedside, checking if he was still breathing. She kept touching his face to feel for warmth and wiping away blood that seeped out of his mouth and nose.

Suddenly at around 6 A.M., Robert's body began trembling. He emerged from the coma in agonizing pain. He had no idea where he was. "I woke up that following morning and saw a ceiling," Robert says. "My last memory was on the soccer field at school, so I thought maybe this was a classroom, but I realized that we did not have a classroom with such a ceiling."

As Robert looked around, he saw his Aunt Dez, a teacher from Lubiri, and several doctors wearing white. He also noticed his soccer uniform covered in blood. "Where am I?" Robert asked. "How did I come here?"

When Robert tried to sit up, his jaw throbbed in terrible pain. Doctors began injecting him with painkillers and rushed him off for an X-ray. He had suffered multiple fractures to his jaw. Doctors performed an operation to seal his jaw shut, after which Robert overheard one of the nurses say, "Wow, that kid is alive? We thought he was dead for sure."

That same morning at the Lubiri school assembly, the headmaster began with an announcement about Robert by saying, "Sad news . . ." Before he could finish, wails rang out throughout the audience from students who thought Robert had died. Then the schoolmaster continued: ". . . you know Robert our soccer player was injured badly and he's admitted at Mulago."

School was cancelled and nearly 100 students made the trek across Kampala to Mulago to see if Robert was still alive. They were surprised to find him awake and in fair condition, although unable to speak because his jaw had been wired shut.

Robert had some friends at school who were born-again Christians and one of them asked him, "Robert, you are so talented, you are a good soccer player, you are a good mathematician, you are the best in class, God has gifted you, so why don't you get saved?"

Another visiting student told him, "We thought you were dead. We just thank God that you are alive. But Robert, do you know why you are still alive? If you had died, where would you have gone? Nobody knows the day, the hour when they will die. Why don't you get saved?"

Robert, who had attended church regularly since his days as a boy in Kiboga but had never taken religion very seriously, pondered those questions for some time. Then he nodded.

"That is when I gave my life to Christ and accepted Christ as my personal savior," Robert says. "Just in case I died, then I could go to Heaven. I was scared to go to Hell. I thought, 'I better do this and be ready because it seems like anytime I can die.'"

Robert's jaw would remain wired shut for a month. He would spend three months in the hospital.

Doctors told Robert he would never play soccer again.

Nine months later, Robert was juggling the ball. He regularly suffered excruciating headaches, but he wasn't about to give up soccer. He couldn't. Soccer sustained him, both emotionally and, more importantly, financially. Soccer was his passion. It was also his job.

After his injury, Aunt Dez couldn't stand by and watch Robert try to nurse himself back to health while living with his grandmother in the slum, so she took Robert home from the hospital, fulfilling a promise to look after him that she, like her cousin Jacent, had made to Nawaguma on her deathbed. Robert stayed with Aunt Dez for five months. Aunt Dez lived in a small but stable house at the edge of the bush in the outskirts of Kampala, where monkeys snuck in from the forest to raid the vegetable garden and could only be turned back by stones thrown by Robert and his three new "sisters." Robert cooked and cleaned the house daily. He worshipped Aunt Dez, who strongly resembled Nawaguma. He even called her "Mama," just as he always did Aunt Jacent.

Robert had missed a full year of school and couldn't return to Lubiri School because Aunt Jacent could no longer afford his tuition there. Jacent offered Robert 100,000 shillings, the equivalent of about $80 at that time, toward a new school.

Progressive Secondary School Bweyogerere was a private school that sought academically gifted students. The registrar there looked at Robert's report forms and offered him a place with a tuition of 180,000 shillings. Robert said he had only 100,000. Then the registrar was informed of Robert's talent on the soccer field, and he was enrolled.

At Progressive, Robert organized a soccer team that competed against other schools for the first time. When second term of S5 arrived, students could campaign for leadership positions, but the school didn't allow day schoolers to participate. The headmaster wouldn't bend the rules but recognized Robert's leadership potential, so he invited him to join the school's boarding section. Robert tied his mattress to a friend's bicycle and walked it five kilometers from Aunt Dez's home to the boarding house. Robert was elected the school's sports minister and was placed in charge of recruiting players, scheduling games, and arranging transportation.

Still, Robert had little money and was often hungry. Sometimes one of the school matrons, another woman who Robert referred to as "Mama," would give him a plate of food from her home within the school grounds. The school's headmaster came to admire Robert so much that he said, "If you lack sugar, come see me." Robert looked forward to visiting days because a friend's family would often invite him to eat with them. Robert never had any visitors on those days, except one afternoon when an uncle stopped by just to verify that Robert was actually attending the school. "My relatives thought I was deceiving them," Robert says. "They thought, 'How can he go to a school that is so expensive and moreover the boarding section?'"

The first time Robert played soccer for Progressive in S5 he led his team to victory in a regional tournament. During his two seasons there he acted as his team's captain, its leading scorer, and also its coach. During a game near the end of the second term of his S6 year, Robert was tripped and fell awkwardly, dislocating his right wrist. He was taken to Mulago Hospital, where doctors planned to operate, but fearing a mistake that could leave him lame, Robert asked instead that they pop the wrist back into place. He planned to rehabilitate it through massage. With his final exams quickly approaching—tests that would determine whether Robert could continue his education at university on a government scholarship—he trained his left hand to write the essays. But when it came time for the exams, he found the left hand to be too slow, so he endured the pain of writing with his right hand. Each time it swelled up, he would shake it out to restore the feeling in his fingers.

During an anxious six-month waiting period to learn his marks, Robert earned money by playing soccer for a club team sponsored by Pepsi. He also did the digging at Aunt Dez's garden, washed cars, and worked as a porter carrying huge loads of bricks up stairs at a building site. He even became an entrepreneur, purchasing a cheap mobile phone and selling calls to people without phones. Finally, Robert returned to Progressive one day to learn his fate and was greeted by fellow students who had already discovered through an announcement at morning assembly that Robert had qualified for a scholarship. When they saw him that day, Robert was mobbed by some of his former soccer team-mates who told him, "Robert, you made it!"

Robert had earned free tuition and room and board at Kampala's Kyambogo University. What Robert did not have was a direction. He didn't know what to do with his life and didn't have anybody to ask. One day during his first term at Kyambogo, Aunt Dez showed up to inform Robert that his father was gravely ill and had come to Kampala. Robert went to visit him. Seeing his father for the first time in more than ten years, Robert felt no emotional connection. Ssemakula barely recognized Robert as one of his many children. Robert suspects that when his father died a few months later, the cause was AIDS. At his father's funeral, it struck Robert how much he lacked a male role model in his life.

"Even though I had rarely seen my dad over the years, I always took some comfort that he was there," Robert says. "His death bothered me a lot. Now I was truly an orphan. At the funeral, I prayed, 'Lord, you are my God, you are my Father. Perhaps you will send someone to help see me through.'"

Shortly after his father's passing, Miracle came. The Miracle Football Club showed up one day to play Robert's Pepsi Club in a friendly match. Miracle played very well that day, but what really captured Robert's attention occurred after the match. The Miracle players invited anyone within earshot to join them for testimony. They said they were recruiting for the Lord. Robert watched carefully as the Miracle players converted people right before his eyes. Afterward he asked some of them if he could get involved with their team. A meeting was arranged with Miracle's coach, Aloysius Kyazze.

Kyazze had once been the captain of the Ugandan national soccer team. A staunch defender. No nonsense. A coach on the field.

"Robert caught my eyes as a coach because I saw in him a great potential as a striker and I passed on whatever I could to help him become a better player, but what impressed me more is that he was very attentive whenever it came to spiritual discipline, devotions, hearing my testimony," Kyazze says. "He didn't ask for anything in exchange like other players who would ask me, 'What will I get? What can I expect?' Robert never thought he would get his daily bread from Miracle. He believed he was there to benefit spiritually, psychologically, and socially and that really touched my heart. I believe he could have played soccer for the national team, but he chose instead to be there for the Lord."

Robert played for Miracle during his two years at Kyambogo University. Because of his studies, he was never able to practice with the team, but in games he was the club's top scorer. He scored in almost every match, sometimes two or three goals, and the team improved significantly with his addition. He was also getting more and more comfortable with the proselytizing after the games and the club's overall brotherhood. "I'll never forget at halftime of one match with Miracle when Aloysius put his hands on my shoulders and drew me close," Robert says. "He was giving me words of encouragement and at that time it felt like I had found a home."

When Robert graduated from Kyambogo at age 20 with a diploma in civil engineering, he had been promised a job with Uganda's National Water Company, because he had done his training there as an engineer. However, when he went to the offices of the National Water Company asking for a job, he was told no positions were available. Once again Robert was homeless. He had to leave his room at the university and didn't want to go back to Aunt Dez's house because there was no steady work there. He had a small allowance from the university for his industrial training, so he was able to rent a room. He owned little more than a cup, a fork, a mattress, and a blanket. After several months, Robert was struggling to find enough money to eat. Following his games with Miracle, Kyazze would give Robert cab fare home and Robert would walk instead so he could afford to buy some food.

On Christmas Eve of 2002, Robert was at a low point. He wanted to visit his Aunt Dez, to be around the closest thing to family that he had left, but he had no money to travel there. He had nothing to eat. Kyazze called him that night and invited Robert to his house. Robert walked three kilometers to Kyazze's home, where he was given a meal and 10,000 shillings as a Christmas gift.

"Sometimes it's embarrassing to describe how far people's lives have fallen when they come to you," Kyazze says. "Robert came when he was almost having nothing, not even a coin for food. It was clear to me that this was a young man who greatly needed help. My heart was there to listen to the issues he was going through and I extended a hand to him because I love to share with people I see as my children."

Robert used some of the money to visit his Aunt Dez's home for Christmas. "The family was having fun and people were drinking beers and they gave me one," Robert says. "As a born-again Christian, I could not drink the beer, but I didn't want them to be unhappy that I wouldn't take the beer, so I kept it. I went home with the bottle of beer because I couldn't throw it out."

It wasn't long before Robert's Christmas money ran out. "I was very hungry and thirsty and I asked myself, 'What can I do?'" Robert says. "I couldn't drink water because I couldn't boil it without kerosene and I couldn't afford to fall sick. I was in a puzzle. Then I saw something. I saw the beer. I said, 'Lord can I take this beer?' I had heard some Christians say that if you are going to die, you do what you must to survive. I sat alone in my room and thought, 'Lord, I'm going to take this beer.' I poured it in my cup and I looked at it for some time. Then I just closed my eyes and swallowed it down. All of it."

The following day Robert recycled his empty beer bottle in exchange for two mangos that would sustain him for the next several days. It was at that point, when Robert had exhausted all of his resources and was beginning to lose hope, that Kyazze told him he wanted Robert to interview for a job with an American ministry called Sports Outreach Institute, an organization that works to provide relief and religion through sports to the world's poorest people. Kyazze worked for Sports Outreach and coached the Good News Football Club, which ministered after games, much like Miracle Football Club. Robert had found his lifeline.

"I saw Robert coming to the position as a raw material which God needed to be prepared," Kyazze says. "He was not a servant at the time he first came to me. No, no, no. He was a young boy. He needed shaping and guidance and direction. When we are called to serve, there must be a process and then later on we ascend."

After nearly a year under Kyazze's tutelage the boy had become a man. Robert had become Katende again. Katende and Kyazze made a good team. The striker and the defender. Kyazze became Katende's mentor. His surrogate father. Kyazze taught him how to teach. Katende would study Kyazze's every move, how he built relationships, his immense patience, how he solved problems. Katende recalls one day during a soccer game when a vicious tackle occurred. Kyazze stopped the game, brought the players together, and made it clear, without raising his voice, that reckless and dangerous play would not be tolerated. Katende admired how whenever Kyazze spoke, he captured the attention of everybody around him. Katende gradually learned how to command that level of respect. Katende also admired Kyazze's extraordinary compassion. On paydays, Kyazze would sometimes slip Katende 3,000 shillings when he knew he was only owed 1,000.

After Katende's training ended in 2003, he was assigned to Katwe to institute a program for children in the slum that involved ministering through soccer. Sports Outreach had designed a blueprint for the project. Kyazze had taught Katende the bullet points, but he'd also stressed that in sports ministry there is room for improvisation. He told Katende that he would have to constantly adjust to the needs of the kids.

Katende had never been to the Nkere district of Katwe where the project would be staged. On his first day there, he arrived with two brand-new red soccer balls provided by Sports Outreach. Walking through the alleyways of the slum carrying those balls, Katende attracted curious children who then followed him to a dump site which had been chosen for a makeshift soccer field. There were only a few children playing at first, but word spread quickly about the coach with the new red balls and before long 60 kids of all ages were showing up every afternoon to play soccer with Katende.

The games were followed by testimony, during which Katende would ask some of the kids to share the challenges they were enduring in their lives, and he would share stories from his own past. At the end of each session Katende distributed to each of the children small pieces of sugarcane, which he paid for from his own pocket. The project was full of street kids. Kids who didn't go to school. Many were orphans. Some were homeless. All of them were desperate for guidance in their own way.

"Some of the kids challenged me initially, but I was certain I could handle any bad behavior because I had lived in the situation they were in," Katende says. "I told them I was not there to judge them, but to love them. I found that if you treated them with respect, you could open up a lot in their hearts. I learned not to always do what I thought was best, but to follow the trend of the children. I thought I was teaching them, but they were also teaching me."

After about a year running the soccer project, Katende was troubled that some kids didn't participate in the games. Ivan Mutesasira was among the children who watched from the sideline every day. At one point Katende asked Ivan, "Why aren't you taking part in the game? No one cares if you are very good. We are just learning."

"Coach," Ivan said. "I fear soccer because I have been hurt before and I could easily break my bones and I don't have the money to take care of my medication."

Katende knew it was time for him to improvise as Kyazze had suggested. "That's when I asked myself, 'These children who are not interested in soccer, how can I involve them?'" Katende says. "I just needed a platform to build a relationship and, like soccer, I needed to be able to play it with them to build that trust stronger."

For about a month, Katende pondered other options. He considered draughts, a Ugandan board game, but it was considered a contest for gamblers. He thought of relay races, but decided that would quickly become monotonous. He thought of basketball, but he didn't have a ball or a goal. When he thought about what he did have available, an idea struck him. A game so foreign that there was no word for it in his native language. An idea so strange that he wondered if it was even possible. "I asked myself, 'Can this really work?'" Katende recalls. "With their education and their environment, can these kids really play this game?"

Chapter 3
Pioneers

Robert Katende teaches children how to play the game in the early days of his chess project. He came to believe chess is the best tool to help slum kids learn how to overcome the many obstacles in their daily lives.

One day after soccer, Katende huddled the children of his Katwe project around him and asked them, "Would you like to learn a new game?"

Katende was pleased to see Ivan Mutesasira and many of the other soccer spectators among the 20 children who gathered.

"What game?" one child asked.

"Chess," Katende said.

There were blank stares. None of the children had ever heard of it.

Then one of them spoke up. "Oh, I know this game," he said. "You chase a person around the compound until you catch him."

"No," Katende said. "*Chess.*"

Katende pulled a vinyl chessboard out of his back pocket and searched for a flat spot on the barren ground of the dump site. Then he produced a plastic bag and emptied its contents onto the board. The children examined the chessboard, counting eight squares on each edge, 64 total, alternating light and dark. They counted out the 32 pieces, 16 black and 16 white. Katende then picked up a knight and asked them what it looks like. "They said it was a goat," Katende recalls. "I told them that it looks like a horse, but they had never seen a horse. So we called it a dog. *Embwa* in Luganda. We were just having fun. They really did not learn anything that first day. I was just trying to capture their imagination so they would come back the following day excited to learn."

The next day's chess session began with one of the children asking, "Coach, how will we ever get to know all of these thirty-two pieces and how they move?"

Katende came up with a plan. He asked the children to group pieces together that looked the same, regardless of color. Six piles were formed. Katende then separated one piece from each pile and told them, "If you learn to move these six pieces, you shall have learned all of the remaining pieces."

The next day he told them the names of each piece, writing each of the names in the dirt for emphasis. Then he asked the kids to choose a piece and share its name. After learning the names, they talked about their positioning on the board. Katende kept the lessons slow. Simple. After soccer each day, he devoted only about 40 minutes to chess to try to avoid any potential burnout. Katende was in no hurry. Where else were these kids going to go?

The next day he started with the pawn. He showed them how a pawn can move forward either one or two spaces on its initial move and then only one space thereafter. Then he asked them to move the pawn and they each took a turn at the board. Finally, one exasperated child said, "Coach, we're just moving pieces around, there is no one who is eating another!"

Katende asked them to be patient. In time they had mastered how a pawn moves and then Katende taught them that it captures not by moving directly forward, but by moving forward one space diagonally.

"Some children tried to capture by moving the pawn the way a pawn is supposed to move and others moved the pawn the way it is supposed to capture," Katende says. "There were a lot of mix-ups."

It took three or four sessions just to cover the movement of the pawn, but to encourage the children, Katende told them that the pawn was the hardest piece to learn, because rules governed its movement that did not apply to any of the other pieces.

Using the pawn as a foundation, Katende taught them how the other pieces move. He told the children that the rook moves like the pawn, but it is not limited in its steps as long as there isn't any other piece in its way, and that it could move either vertically or horizontally.

Then Katende explained that the knight moves like the rook, except that it is limited to only two steps and then it turns for a single step. Knowing that the knight could be a frustrating piece for the children to understand, Katende created a phrase that the children eventually translated into a sort of dance step. *One-Two-Turn. One-Two-Turn.* Katende challenged them and eventually all of the students wanted to move the knight without showing the other kids that they had counted the steps. Katende then placed one black knight and one white pawn on the board and asked all of the children to try to capture the pawn with the knight.

"That was a good puzzle," Katende says. "It triggered them to think, one-two-turn, one-two-turn. The pawn was always there stationary, but how many times must you move the knight until it reaches the pawn? They might get right beside the pawn and then they fear moving away from it. It was a struggle, but eventually they mastered it."

Katende told them that the bishop is the only religious person on the board and they translated it into Luganda. *Munadiini.* It was easier to explain the bishop moving diagonally and always on the same color, because the piece moves very much the same way as the king in draughts, a game many of the children had previously played. The ones who knew taught the ones who did not know as Katende sat back and watched.

Learning the queen was simple. Katende took a bishop in one hand and a rook in the other and told them that the queen combines the movements of both pieces.

The day Katende reached for the final piece, the king, the children expected the king to be moving in an extraordinary way because of its size relative to the other pieces. Then Katende explained that the king could move only one space in any direction. When he sensed some disappointment among his pupils, he related the story of the king to their lives.

"I asked them, 'Who knows the Kabaka of Buganda and who has ever seen him running?'" Katende says. "No one had ever seen him running. I said, 'No, this is a very powerful person. He's a king. He does not run. He's a diplomat. He just takes one step here and he's through with his movement.' They knew that the Kabaka does not run because he's a powerful person respected by everyone. They saw the king in a new way."

As Katende spent weeks painstakingly explaining each of the pieces, the number of children in attendance dropped. "One kid called Gerald after twenty minutes of each session he would be dozing with saliva coming out of his mouth," Katende recalls. "I would ask him if he was okay and he always snapped awake. By this point we had lost some kids because they saw learning chess as a long process."

The original group of 20 children eventually dwindled to only five boys. For several weeks, attendance even dropped as low as three and Katende wondered if his suspicions had been correct all along. *Can these kids really play this game?* He questioned if the chess project could survive.

After Katende had covered all of the pieces, the three remaining children convinced the two who had recently dropped out to return. When they came back, Katende asked the boys who knew how to move all of the pieces to teach the others. When the attendance finally stabilized at five, Ivan Mutesasira, Samuel Mayanja, Gerald Mutyaba, Julius Ssali, and Richard Tugume, Katende began referring to them as "The Pioneers." The Pioneers called Katende "Coach Robert."

"The Pioneers developed a very great interest in the game," Richard Tugume says. "Time came when we reduced our time of going to soccer because we really loved chess so very much. We saw how this game could develop our minds."

Katende identified Richard as a leader. Richard had been playing soccer on the dump site the day Katende first arrived to stage the soccer portion of his sports ministry there. Richard was among the first to join Katende's soccer project and had rarely missed a day since. One evening, in an effort to help empower Richard, Katende handed the boy the project's only chessboard to take home with him. Richard quickly gave it back.

"But why?" Katende asked. "Why don't you want to keep our board?"

Richard remained quiet until Katende pulled him aside and asked him again why he didn't want to keep the board.

"I am sorry, Coach," Richard said, "but when Daddy comes back home every evening he is drunk and he fights with Mommy and he will end up destroying our board."

Instead, that same day Richard rallied the rest of the Pioneers to search the dump site for bottle caps and a blank piece of cardboard. They drew the 64 squares on the cardboard and carefully shaded every other one and then etched the names of the 32 pieces on the bottle caps. For many evenings thereafter when it came time for Katende to leave Katwe, the Pioneers played their new favorite game, with bottle caps on cardboard, until it was too dark to see.

Coach Robert never had a coach. He figured out chess on his own simply by watching some of his friends play it in the schoolyard during his second year at Lubiri Secondary School.

"I saw students playing this strange game and I asked them, 'What is this?'" Katende says. "They told me that the game was only for guys who are really clever. I had to prove I was clever enough for this game."

Katende would watch his schoolmates play every evening and eventually asked if he could join them. He bought a cheap vinyl chessboard and pieces from a friend and played recreationally on and off for the next few years. He didn't really play chess competitively until he reached the engineering department at Kyambogo University, where he competed in tournaments against far more talented players who had grown up in affluent families playing the game more consistently. Throughout the odyssey of his childhood, one of the few possessions Katende held on to was the chess set he had purchased during secondary school, and it was that same set he brought with him to teach the children of Katwe.

Katende had learned the game primarily through trial and error and he taught it that way to the Pioneers. He admits that he didn't even know all of the rules of the game until several months into the chess project when a friend from Sports Outreach gave him a book titled

Chess for Beginners. The book taught Katende some basic chess strategy and tactics. He learned the importance of controlling the central part of the board to gain a position of strength. While he had been taught "castling," a move where the king and rook exchange positions, the book taught him "long castling" and "short castling" and that a player should try to castle within the first ten moves of the game. He also discovered that chess could be divided into three stages: opening, middlegame, and endgame. "Reading that book was a turning point," Katende says. "I studied every word and then I used it as a reference to teach the children some things about the game that I was just learning myself."

Working without any depth of knowledge in chess theory, which is a means of approaching a game more as a whole than as a series of individual moves, Katende taught his students to analyze the board and try to make the best choice for each move. At first they all wanted to use every move to capture, whether it made sense for the long-term result or not. They thought only one move at a time. So Katende gradually taught them to plan, to think one move ahead, then two, then three, and beyond.

"I don't like the way players who say they have learned chess by theory make moves and they can't explain why they have even made those moves," Katende says. "My players must have a reason why they play each move. It might be a bad reason, but at least there's a reason."

Katende taught them to play one piece at a time. The Pioneers' first games involved only pawns. After they learned the rook, the four rooks were added to the board for play. "At first I just had them move any color piece they wanted to as long as they move it the way it's supposed to move," Katende says. "I didn't concern myself with white then black then white then black. White might make ten moves in a row without black making a single move. Someone might move the queen right beside the opposing king. Then some moves later the king might capture the queen. It wasn't very strict. I just wanted to see if they could move the pieces correctly and let them discover things slowly."

For the first few months, the Pioneers thought the game ended when one player captured all of his opponent's pieces. Then when Katende felt the Pioneers were ready, he explained that the game is actually won when an opponent's king is hopelessly cornered in "checkmate," which begins with the warning that that king is in "check," or what Katende called "target."

"It was an interesting moment for them when they first learned about their king in target," Katende says. "At first it was like a big scare. Their breathing rate changed. 'Where can I run? What can I do?'"

Initially the children struggled with the idea that the king didn't actually need to be captured for the game to end. Then Katende explained checkmate with another story to which the Pioneers could relate.

"The children would always ask me, 'Why should I tell you your king is in target when I can just capture your king?'" Katende says. "I told them, 'No, you don't kill the president. The president is just arrested. Who has ever heard of a president being killed? He's a big person in the country. You only arrest him. Target is like you're telling a president, "You are in danger. Do you have any soldiers to protect you?" If he doesn't, then you arrest him and the game is over.'"

To further illustrate his point, Katende demonstrated what is known as "The Fool's Mate," which he'd learned from *Chess for Beginners*. The term refers to a series of simple moves at the opening of a game that can quickly checkmate an opponent.

Eventually Katende began playing against the Pioneers, usually rotating them through the seat opposite him, sometimes letting them team up to decide each of their moves, but always explaining why he made each of his moves and thoroughly evaluating each move made by the opponent as the children looked on with rapt attention. Katende was always searching for ways to challenge them.

"One time I was teaching them how to win when you have just two bishops and a king and your opponent just has a king," Katende says. "I did not tell them what to do. I just asked them, 'Who of you can checkmate me when I just have a king?' We played for over fifty moves and they failed to mate me. They said, 'Coach, it is not possible.' I told them that it is possible and I left it to them to figure out how. They discovered it by themselves."

As months passed, the chess project began to expand slightly beyond the Pioneers, possibly caused by word of mouth that the sugarcane had turned into a daily bowl of porridge. Katende began to realize the profound lessons the chessboard had for his congregation of children. They were slum kids. He was a slum kid. Their story was his story. They had all been in target for their entire lives.

"I came to appreciate that chess is the best tool for kids in the slums," Katende says. "I believe when they play the game they can integrate the principles used in the game into their daily life. The moment your opponent makes a move, it is like posing a challenge to you, and the whole issue is to think, 'What can I do to overcome this?' It is like the challenges they face every day. They must think how they can overcome those as well. I told them they can never resign in a game, never give up until they are checkmated. That is where the chessboard is like life. That is the magic in the game."

Before long it became harder and harder to differentiate the chess games from the spiritual guidance that followed. A teaching point could spring up anytime. Whenever Katende saw a player become frustrated during a game, he would share the biblical story of Joseph:

"Joseph was in a family with his brothers and though he was not a bad behaved person, in a way they mistreated him. They ended up even selling him off to go and work as a slave. If Joseph were looking for someone to blame he would definitely be on wrong terms with his brothers, but this was God's plan. He went through all of that suffering, but it was a connection to another level. You need to develop that positivity in you so that problems do not affect you greatly. With every challenge you need to see what is the lesson out of this? Why has God allowed this to happen? How does He want me to grow from this? Is it endurance? Is it tolerance?

You must develop that muscle to stand and know how to address it when something bad happens to you."

Whenever there was a crisis of confidence, Katende would tell his favorite story about an inept doctor.

"Think of a situation when you are sick and you have gone to the clinic for treatment and a doctor comes up and says, 'Young man, you're sick. I am going to inject you, but I don't know whether I still remember how to inject. Let me first see if I can remember.' Then he gets a sponge and he tries to inject it and says, 'I think I can remember. Okay, let's do the injection.' Can you allow yourself to be injected? Of course you can't. Why? Because the doctor does not believe in himself. Then how do you entrust your life to him? You cannot. If you don't believe in yourself, how do you expect anyone else to believe in you?"

Katende's lessons were designed to bond a bunch of desperate slum children into a community of chess players helping each other learn how to see into the future.

"Someday you will be able to read your opponent's mind many moves in advance," Katende told them. "You will see what is going to happen on the chessboard before it happens. You are all going to be prophets."

Brian Mugabi sat among them on that very first day when Katende placed the chessboard in the dirt and spilled the pieces over it. Brian had been playing in the soccer project from the beginning when he was about 11 years old, sneaking away from his chores whenever he could, at the risk of a caning from his mother. He was relatively small and sometimes grew frustrated playing soccer against boys who were bigger and stronger and more skilled. He kept coming, less for the soccer and more to hear what the young coach had to say, and, of course, for the food.

Brian embraced chess from the first day, because he recognized immediately that his size didn't matter. This game was contested with the brain and Brian thought there could be nobody better at plotting and scheming. He saw chess as a chance to be good at something for the first time in his life. The game reminded him of the days when his father took him to the video halls and he watched movies about soldiers on horseback with spears charging toward one another. The idea had always fascinated him. One army against another. Do or die. That's what he saw when he looked at the chessboard.

Brian escaped to the chess project whenever possible during its first several months, long enough to have learned how each of the soldiers attacked and captured, but not yet how to command his army successfully as a whole. One night after chess as he was walking home through Katwe, he was struck by a bicycle. Brian was knocked down and badly hurt. He had to be carried home and that night he noticed blood in his urine. The following day he was taken to the hospital, where doctors discovered he was bleeding internally. He was treated there for a week. As Brian was laid up in his family's shack recuperating, he couldn't stop thinking about returning to the chess project, seeing his friends again, reconnecting with the first sense of stability he'd ever experienced. He began to realize it wasn't the game that he craved as much as the people who played it with him. It would be three months before Brian recovered enough to return to the chess project, by which time Katende had dubbed some of the other boys he had first trained with "The Pioneers."

By that time, Katende had arranged to have the chess project moved from the dump site to a dusty veranda outside Bishop John Michael Mugerwa's office, where a roof would protect the children from the rain and enough dim light shone to allow them to continue playing on those evenings when dusk fell early over the slum. One day, probably in 2005, as Brian snuck away from his younger siblings, Phiona and

Richard, and darted off to the chess project, he had no idea that he was blazing a trail and he could never have imagined where that trail might eventually lead. He certainly didn't know anyone was there when Katende spotted somebody at the edge of the veranda peeking around the corner.

A young girl.

Chapter 4
Resurrection

Phiona Mutesi prays inside her family's shack
before leaving for her three-hour trek through
the treacherous alleyways of Katwe to fetch
fresh water.

"I have no memory of my father," Phiona says. "I was so young I didn't even know how he died. After his funeral we stayed in the village for a few weeks and one morning when I woke up, my older sister Juliet told me she was feeling a headache. We got some herbs and gave them to her and then she went to sleep. The following morning we found her dead in the bed. That is what I remember."

Only God knows what day the child was born. There is no birth certificate. No documentation of any kind. They don't bother with that kind of paperwork at a clinic in Katwe. Many Africans trace their birthdays back to nothing more specific than a certain year marked by a landmark in their country's history. In Uganda, many people track their birthdays to a war. Harriet believes her third daughter was born in 1996, but she doesn't know her daughter's birthday and doesn't understand why anyone would need to know, because nobody celebrates birthdays in the slum.

Because she is illiterate, Harriet didn't bestow a name upon her newborn daughter, so much as a sound. Harriet's cousin, Milly Nanteza, had given all of her children names beginning with an *F* sound. Harriet liked that. Nanteza had named one of her daughters with the sound *FEE-OH-NUH*. It was never spelled out. When Harriet is asked how her daughter's name is spelled, she does not understand the question. The answer would not be determined in any official manner for many years.

Phiona was about three years old when her father died and her life turned upside down. She had been preparing to go to kindergarten. Suddenly she was no longer a child but a worker. The widowed Harriet needed all of her children to be part of her labor force.

By the time Harriet had returned home from Buyubu after the second family funeral she'd endured in three weeks, she had lost her job at the New African Child School and the family had been evicted from their home on Salaama Road. Night and Brian, who were about 13 and six years old, respectively, dropped out of school to help support the family. "After my husband's death I had so many children and I could not pay the rent," Harriet says. "Life was so, so, so terrible. I could not pay for their school fees and they were denied exams or report forms. Eventually I had to make a choice to either educate my children or to feed them."

One day after seeing a child walking through the slum selling boiled maize from a saucepan on her head, Harriet, believing she had no other choice, decided her family would do the same. Each morning she would walk to the Kibuye outdoor market and buy some maize, often on borrowed money. Harriet would then cook it and she and her children would wander around selling it in the slum.

"At times you could grow weary because you are walking long distances with the maize on your head without anyone buying," Brian says. "And personally I had bad feelings about what we were doing. We all wanted to be in school. It would come to around 5 P.M. and at that time most of my friends would be playing and I wanted to go and join them, but that is a time that our mother would tell us to go and sell the maize."

Beginning when Phiona was about five years old, Harriet sent her daughter out alone into the slum each day carrying a saucepan of maize on her head. She would sell during morning and evening teas. Phiona carried 20 corncobs and each was to be sold for 100 shillings (U.S. $.06), a supply worth 2,000 shillings, but a five-year-old girl rarely returned with that.

"There were some moments when you would come across some

street children and they would beat you up and steal your maize and then they go," Phiona says. "At times they would even take the money you have so far earned and you go home with nothing. It was really very challenging because I could go home crying and I could not express anything to my mother because she is also feeling very bad about that and she is preparing to cane me. So it was such a terrible moment. That really affected us because when we were unable to raise enough money, we would end up not eating that day."

There were plenty of days when Harriet had no food for her children. They usually ate no breakfast in the morning. At times Harriet was able to scrape together some rice for a meal at midday. A cup of tea often would have to suffice as dinner. Whenever there wasn't enough food for the entire family, Harriet would fast. Once a year, on Christmas Day, Harriet allowed her children to skip selling maize and she would buy meat for their daily meal, which she would split among them while taking none for herself. Christmas was the only day of the year the children were permitted to eat until they were full.

Before her first run of maize each day, Phiona was expected to do much of the housework that her sister Juliet had once done. She was also required to fetch water. Phiona would wake up at five o'clock each morning to begin a three-hour roundtrip trek through Katwe to fill a jerry can with drinkable water. Sometimes she would even sling an extra jug over her shoulder for a neighbor in exchange for a few shillings she could give to her mother for food.

"We fetched water, sold maize, and did chores," Phiona says. "That was our day. In most cases we used to come back and we were really tired and our mother realized this and she used to help us to even wash our clothes because we were too tired to do that ourselves."

Understanding the value of the education that she could never get as a child, Harriet tried repeatedly to reenroll her children in school, but she could never keep up with the fees. She transferred them from school to school, but they were typically expelled before completing a full term. During a period of six years, Phiona completed less than two grades of school. Even when they were enrolled, Phiona and her siblings continued to sell maize in the evenings.

As she grew older, Phiona's behavior began to change. She would often fight with children around the neighborhood. Unlike most girls, she would even stand up to the boys. One time a boy teased her about how she had no father and her family slept on the ground and Phiona attacked him so aggressively that Harriet had to break up the fight before Phiona hurt the boy.

"I would do all sorts of bad things," Phiona says. "I would run around with the wild kids in the neighborhood abusing whoever we find. I did not even fear to quarrel with older people if anybody did anything that was not in line with what I wanted. I usually had nobody around telling me what to do and what not to do, so I wound up learning a lot of bad actions."

Phiona attributes her poor conduct to her family's constant state of desperation. "It affected us to a certain extent, but our mother used to encourage us so we didn't lose hope," Phiona says. "Many times the landlord would come to our home demanding his money for rent and we had no money even for food. Everything was really in a mess so we were really very much scared and we didn't know what was next."

When she is asked if there were any happy moments in her childhood during that time, Phiona shakes her head and for emphasis she responds in English: "No."

In her mind it would be best if it happened by car. Harriet wasn't exactly sure where or when, but that would be a quick way to go. It wouldn't require any planning, just a snap decision. A brief jolt of courage, or perhaps cowardice, and she would be gone.

"The life I was leading, I was fed up with it," Harriet says. "I had so many challenges and at times I lost hope. During that time for sure I had nothing in mind apart from looking for food to make us survive and I always wondered if God would ever remember us. I was so tired of living that kind of life. I was working very hard but all in vain. It was a real devil distressing me. It caused me to hate myself and I felt like it wasn't worth living. So time came when I said, 'Why don't I die and leave this kind of life?'"

Only her responsibility to her children had prevented Harriet from committing suicide. She would always think of them and wonder what would happen to them without her. In her most despondent moments she wondered if she wouldn't rather die than see her kids suffering. She wanted to let them go. At some point in Katwe, Harriet Nakku approached that dark point of no return when she began to think, "Could my children really be any worse off without me?"

Sometime around the year 2000, about a year after the death of her husband and daughter, a friend who was worried about Harriet's state of mind directed her to see a pastor. "Before 2000 I had a dream over and over and a voice spoke to me, 'Why don't you get saved?'" Harriet says. "But I would not pay attention."

That day Harriet confessed Christ as her savior. She was born-again. Then the pastor shared a prophecy.

Says Harriet, "When I went to church and I saw that man of God, he spoke to me and he said, 'You have been praying to God that a vehicle can hit you and you die. You go today and God will indicate something to you.'"

Later that afternoon, as Harriet was walking through Katwe carrying her infant, Richard, near a place called Prayer Palace, she heard a car speeding around a bend in the road and it was headed directly toward her. The onlookers in Katwe that day drew in a collective gasp, certain they were about to witness yet another senseless death in the slum. Harriet said a quick prayer and braced for the impact.

"The vehicle came and suddenly stopped right where we are," Harriet says. "I saw the motorcar turning around and then facing where it had come from and I remembered the prophecy and realized that the man of God was referring to me. Maybe it was God's arrangement. I cannot explain that."

That single day changed Harriet's entire outlook on her life.

"At that time my heart was transformed," Harriet says. "I used to spend most of the time crying and worried before I got saved. Then I became strong and I gained hope and inner peace. Our situation was not all that good, but I began to meditate on what God had done for us, somehow keeping us alive. I wouldn't be here anymore if it wasn't for the power of God. And I thank him for that."

The first time Phiona died she was about seven years old. It happened suddenly one evening. Phiona fell sick with a fever and then she was gone. Her body was cold and still. Nobody could find a pulse.

Phiona's body was dressed for burial and cotton was placed in each nostril to stem any flow of blood. As is custom in Uganda, the family removed all of the possessions from the shack, placed the body in the center of the floor, and invited the neighbors to sit on mats along the walls and help the family mourn and pray for the deceased. Harriet went to church to solicit some funds for Phiona's body to be transported to the village for a funeral, while Phiona's youngest siblings were sequestered outside the shack unaware of what had occurred.

Several hours after Phiona had died, Night began to notice some sweating around her sister's legs. Before long, Phiona's entire body appeared to be perspiring, so Night removed some of the clothes she had put on her sister. By the time Harriet had returned from church, Phiona had resurrected. "Personally, I've never seen anything like that," Harriet says. "Even though the child was mine, I really feared her. I don't like even to talk about that, because I know people will be fearing her. For sure, there is no way I can explain that. It is God's glory. At that time, I was just praying and believing God, but I was not even praying for her to be brought back to life. I don't even know what happened to bring her back to life, but I believe there is a reason for it."

"All of a sudden we saw Phiona returning to life and all of the visitors scattered and ran out of the room because they believed this is a ghost," Night says. "We were also fearing her. We thought she was a ghost. Then our mother said, 'No, it is God who has brought back my daughter.' We went ahead and told Phiona, 'You were dead.' Phiona told us, 'No, I was just asleep.' She became better, but people feared her for some good time."

Some of the neighbors who had mourned Phiona that night refused to make any further contact with her and began referring to her as "the girl who feared the grave."

About a year later, Phiona died again. She fell gravely ill and Harriet begged one of her sisters for the money to take Phiona to the hospital. While Harriet was never informed of a diagnosis, she believes her daughter had an acute case of malaria, a malady that is contracted with the frequency of the common cold in Katwe, and which Phiona had endured many times before. Phiona lost consciousness and fluid had to be removed from her spine. Harriet was informed that her daughter's condition was life-threatening. "I was so terrified," Harriet says. "I was told that when someone gets some water removed from their spinal cord the chances are very small that they are going to survive. I knew Phiona was going to die, just like Juliet before her."

Harriet left Night at Phiona's bedside because she was so certain of Phiona's fate and could not bear the thought of losing another daughter. She took Brian and Richard with her to try to gather the money to bury Phiona. Several days later, Phiona baffled her doctors by making a sudden recovery.

"I was very surprised that Phiona stabilized," Harriet says. "Maybe her time had not yet come. That must have been God's plan. I believe there is divine intervention in my daughter's life."

Says Phiona, "I don't remember anything about that time except that when I came home my mother told me, 'You died for two days.'"

Harriet had lost everything that belonged to her, except for her children and a mattress. Now the mattress was gone. Harriet had offered her mattress as collateral for a loan, seed money for a job selling cassava in the Kibuye market. When the business failed within a week, the mattress was gone. Harriet and her children had nothing left to sleep on.

At that point they had moved in with Harriet's mother, into a tiny shack in Katwe barely fit for one person but sleeping six. One day the landlord showed up and told them that without a rent payment, they would have to leave immediately. They had no money.

So the family moved to another shack in the Kizungu zone which borders Katwe, a dwelling that had been abandoned because it was in such a decrepit state. Shortly after they arrived there, Harriet's mother died. They continued to stay there despite returning one day to find that their possessions had been stolen because they could not afford a lock for the door. Finally, the house collapsed. At that time, Harriet didn't have money to rent another house, so she begged her stepbrother, Juma Sserunkuma, to allow her family to stay with him in the two-room shack he rented in the nearby Nateete slum.

Harriet didn't know until they arrived there that Sserunkuma practiced witchcraft. On some nights Sserunkuma would wake up Harriet and the children at 3 A.M. and insist that they go outside while he performed rituals like slaughtering a chicken and spreading its blood around the shack. Sserunkuma constantly claimed that someone was urinating in his bedroom, even though he kept it locked. He would complain that he was no longer getting the money he used to earn and that Harriet's presence precluded him from obtaining a wife. "He would tell me that everything of his was in a mess," Harriet says. "There were some flowers he would irrigate with local brew and they all dried up. It seems he thought that we had disorganized his spirits."

Sserunkuma eventually ordered Harriet and her family to leave. "I told my children that it was not safe for us to stay with him," Harriet says. "I feared he could sacrifice us, slaughter us, so we had to leave his place and go on the street."

Because she had no other choice, Harriet and her children stayed on the roadside near the Kibuye market. The only other option for shelter was back in her father's village in Seeta, but Harriet didn't have the fare to transport everybody there and wasn't sure she'd even be welcome. "During that time when we slept on the street, I didn't know that we would ever be able to get another house to stay in," Phiona says. "We were sleeping in the road and people were laughing at us. Our mother's plan was for us to sometime go back to the village."

Day after day on the roadside, Harriet split a single cassava among her children while she fasted on water. Harriet survived on small donations from friends in the church, who eventually persuaded her that living in the street wasn't safe for the children and that she should take her family to sleep in the church once it had emptied each evening.

At that dire moment, the solution fell to Night. She left the family on the roadside and made a decision she'd been resisting for a long time, the same decision her mother once made in a similar moment of hopelessness. "I had to go and get a man and I started staying with that man," Night says. "So when I got that man, it wasn't the right thing to do because really I was not of age. I was fifteen years old. But I had no option and he was the one now giving me some money to support my family. So that's how God rescued us from the street."

After three weeks on the roadside, with a gift of 40,000 shillings from the man with whom Night was staying, Harriet rented a room in the nearby Masajja district, where the family stayed for four months until that structure was demolished because the landlord wanted to build a sounder structure. So once again Harriet moved her family to yet another shack in Katwe, the sixth time they had relocated in five years.

To help muster the rent for each of these humble dwellings, Harriet returned to work at the Kibuye market, a chaotic outdoor bazaar that offers everything from vegetables to underwear to toothpaste to dishes, much of which sits in the mud inside an entrance marked by cattle defecating in the street.

Harriet didn't give up after her first business failure at the market, but tried again after learning from her mistakes. She no longer sold cassava, which had proven to be expensive and had a short shelf life, instead choosing to sell curry powder, which was far cheaper and more durable.

Harriet would eventually expand her inventory to tea leaves, avocados, and eggplants, which she normally sells from a wobbly wooden stand under a feeble umbrella that offers virtually no protection from the blistering sun. Six days a week she leaves her home at 2 A.M. to make a five-kilometer walk to meet the farmers who bring their goods into Kampala for purchase, and then she resells those goods for a tiny profit that she hopes will amount to enough money each month to pay rent and feed her children a daily meal of rice.

Because of her work schedule, Harriet is usually gone from the family's shack and her children never know when she will return. Harriet sometimes passes several days without seeing them. "When I wake up in the morning I commit my kids to God's hands," she says. "I don't always know where my kids are. God is like their father."

One day when it came time to go out on the evening run selling maize, Brian was nowhere to be found. Before his accident with the bicycle he had begun a routine of wandering off at about the same time each day. Curious, his little sister would try to follow him. But Phiona would inevitably lose her big brother among the labyrinth of alleys in Katwe. She couldn't keep up with him.

But on this day, perhaps motivated by the possibility of finding a meal on a day when she'd had nothing to eat, Phiona was able to track Brian for five kilometers, all the way to an abandoned lot, a dump site that was being used as a soccer field. Phiona looked on from a safe distance as Brian began to play soccer with a group of boys, watched over by a young coach. She studied the coach and liked the way he joined in the game and seemed to genuinely care for the children. After about an hour, the soccer game ended. Brian and the other boys then walked deeper into the valley of Katwe, toward the heart of Nkere. Phiona continued to follow her brother until at one point a boy named Gerald turned, saw Phiona, and said, "Brian, your sister is coming."

Brian retreated to where Phiona was standing and insisted she go home. After initially resisting, Phiona turned and began to walk back toward home, but then turned again and continued her stealthy pursuit of her brother until she reached a dusty veranda across the alley from the shack of Hakim Ssewaya. Brian disappeared inside. Phiona carefully peeked around a corner to see where he had gone.

"I saw there were many children seated and they were all looking at some good things and I didn't know if it was a game because I had never seen it," Phiona says. "I looked at it some more and I just felt like I really wanted to go inside and touch the beautiful pieces. I thought, 'What could make all these kids so silent?' Then I watched them play the game and get happy and excited and I wanted a chance to be that happy."

Phiona kept peering around the corner, fascinated by the game. Suddenly she was spotted by the coach. "Young girl," said Katende. "Don't be afraid. You come."

Chapter 5
Teach Her What You Know

Gloria Nansubuga was four when Robert Katende selected her to become
nine-year-old Phiona Mutesi's first chess tutor.

Phiona," she responded, when Katende asked her name. But he couldn't hear her. Nobody could. She spoke at a whisper with her chin buried in her chest. Katende took a step closer. "Phiona," she said again, no louder.

She was dirty. Her skirt was soaking wet. Her blouse torn. Her bare feet caked in mud. She stunk.

She gradually eased her way onto the veranda, where many boys and a few girls were sitting on wooden benches or the floor, playing the strange game. She picked up a queen and caressed it with her fingers. Phiona had never felt anything like it.

The other children in the chess project did not welcome the new kid. Brian wasn't quite sure how to handle his sister among them. Even Katende stood back strategically to see if the community would embrace her without his influence. Phiona ate her bowl of porridge alone. Everybody refused to sit near her because of her stench. They laughed at her. They told her to leave. "Look at the dirty girl," one said. "You girl, you go away. You're not worthy to be with us here. We can't be with such a dirty girl."

Suddenly the quiet girl became more aggressive. Phiona walked over toward her primary tormentors with a bearing that she was ready to fight. The moment is what Katwe had trained Phiona for; an animalistic awareness that each day is survival of the fittest, that retaliation is demanded, that even the most naturally timid creature must fight when her existence depends on it. Phiona could sense that this day was a benchmark in her young life, a line drawn in the dust, and she could not, would not, be turned away from the beautiful pieces.

"They abused me, but they didn't know who they were joking with because I also abused them," Phiona says. "I said so many bad words. I told them, 'Look at your nose. Look at your teeth. You are not so good-looking, either.'"

Phiona threatened some of the other children until Katende and Brian stepped in to break them up. Brian dragged his sister off the veranda and walked her back to their shack, where he told their mother about how Phiona had quarreled with the other children and how much he hated to see his sister abused like that. "Our mother got angry with me and she even slapped me for my behavior," Phiona says. "She told me never to go there again."

On his way home that night, Robert Katende believed he had seen the last of Phiona Mutesi. "Because the day was so hard for her, for sure I did not expect to meet her again," Katende says. "When she came back the next day, I knew she had an enduring kind of spirit. I knew this girl had courage."

She may have come back for the porridge, but she came. The following day Phiona cleverly waited for the moment when her mother left their home for church and then sprinted to the chess project. She had rinsed herself with water and dressed in clothes that she had freshly cleaned in the wash basin. Luckily for her, Brian was not at the veranda that day.

Phiona was greeted by Katende, who scanned the room seeking a candidate to help tutor the new girl. He knew that her mentor must be another female, because none of the boys would deign to teach a brand-new girl, but there was only one other girl at the project that day: a four-year-old who knew nothing more than some basics about how to move the pieces. Katende introduced nine-year-old Phiona to the tiny girl and then said to the younger one, "Gloria, teach her what you know."

Gloria Nansubuga had been with the program for only a short time, convinced to join at the insistence of her older brother, Benjamin, if for no other reason than to get a free meal.

Initially, Gloria did not want to tutor Phiona, and Phiona did not want Gloria to tutor her. "I'm teaching an old lady," Gloria would complain. Phiona was embarrassed by the age difference as well.

"I thought to myself, 'How could this tiny girl teach me anything?'" Phiona says. "Whenever Gloria taught me, I really felt as if she was putting me down. But as much as I was despising her, I enjoyed what she was doing, because I wanted to learn the game."

Phiona eventually grew to feel comfortable around Gloria, who was the only girl in the project who seemed to accept her. "Whenever I assigned her to Gloria, Phiona could feel peace and she knew she was going to learn," Katende says. "It became a driving force for Phiona that if this young girl is able to learn the game, then she can also learn. Phiona could not be as comfortable with me as sometimes she was with Gloria. With Gloria she could ask four or five times until she understood something. With me she would fear to ask me so many times one thing."

Gloria showed Phiona the oddly shaped pieces and explained how each was regulated by different rules about how it could move. The pawns. The rooks. The bishops. The knights. The king. And finally the queen, the most powerful piece on the board. She told Phiona about the *embwa* and the *munadiini,* and about how the Kabaka, the king, is never killed but simply arrested, although Gloria didn't totally understand yet how that translated to the game. Gloria told Phiona that the most important point in many chess games is when a pawn reaches the opponent's back row, how it was called "queening," and how at that moment a pawn miraculously transforms into a queen. How could Phiona have imagined at the time how these 32 pieces and 64 squares could queen her?

What made Phiona come back day after day were the beautiful pieces that had attracted her in the first place. She desperately wanted to move these pieces just as the other children were moving them. She could see the excitement in their faces, but at first she was not feeling the same emotion. After several weeks under Gloria's tutelage, Phiona began to understand the basic strategy of the game. At one point, Phiona heard one of the other children tell her, "Ah, that was a great move." She felt happy and wanted to make more and more great moves, positive reinforcement being an unfamiliar but powerful incentive to a slum child.

"Phiona really grasped the game so easily," Gloria says. "Nothing disturbed her. When she started learning, she developed a very big interest in the game and she constantly continued to play and that's how she became better."

As the two became friends, Gloria also mentored Phiona about her conduct outside of the game.

Says Phiona, "One time when I got upset with Gloria, she told me, 'Phiona, don't abuse me. Coach Robert told us that the people who play chess are always good people. They are very well disciplined. They don't make trouble.' In a way Gloria was bringing out a very good lesson to me."

After about two months of training with Gloria, Phiona had caught up to her four-year-old tutor. Gloria had nothing left to teach, and Katende knew it was time for Phiona to move on to the opposite side of the veranda, to start actually playing the game, and to do it at a level of competition that had caused many other girls to flee from the program. It was time to start playing with the boys.

Ivan Mutesasira was about eight years old when his mother, Annet Nakiwala, told him and his four siblings that it was time to go. Nakiwala loaded all of her possessions onto her head and, trailed by her children, walked away from her husband and out into Katwe, vowing never to speak to him again.

"I never got to know what caused the divorce, because by then I was very young," Ivan says. "I remember seeing our mother carrying her things away from our home and she told us to follow her. We were five young kids and we did not know what was going on."

Nakiwala and her children relocated to another shack in Katwe, but she could not afford to raise five kids on her own. The family struggled to find food and their living conditions were miserable. "The place where we stayed, the water would come inside the room whenever it rained," Ivan says. "I could not even sleep at night because I had to be awake to be able to lift things from wherever the water level has reached and continue to put them upwards. Sometimes I could spend two days without sleep."

Like so many other kids in Katwe, Ivan bounced in and out of school because of lack of funds. "We faced several challenges that included starving at school because we were not paying the feeding fee so we could not eat," Ivan says. "I remember some days we could offer to go to wash the school saucepans and then we could eat what is left not eaten from the saucepans and the teachers' dishes."

Eventually Ivan dropped out of school in P7 and remained out of school for three years. Five years after she had taken Ivan from his father, with no other choice, Nakiwala sent him back. Ivan was another child of Katwe, blowing in the wind, when one day in 2003 his friend Richard Tugume told him he had met a coach who had come to Katwe with real soccer balls that they could use to play.

"At first we thought that Coach Robert had come for a short term because there were other people who used to come with those good balls, but always after a short while they would leave," says Ivan, who believes he is 20 years old. "We didn't know that he was serious to stay, but later we realized that he was really committed to us, that he was different from all of the others."

As one of the Pioneers, one the oldest players in the project and one of the few who was humble and well behaved from the outset, Ivan was identified by Katende as another potential leader. But Ivan lacked self-esteem, so Katende sought to empower him by calling on him to tutor younger players. Whenever Katende identified a new player with talent, he placed him with Ivan. One day Katende introduced Ivan to Benjamin Mukumbya and told Ivan, "Teach him what you know."

Benjamin was a street kid. A loner. As a young child, he used to be left at home alone all day while both of his parents scrounged Katwe for a few shillings to feed him. Then one day after thieves robbed the family's shack, Benjamin's mother, Jane Kobugabe, brought her son to stay at an aunt's place in a nearby village. Benjamin was not fed properly there and at one point when his mother discovered him gravely malnourished, she took him back to Kampala, where he fell victim to negative influences. "Actually, my father was not a Christian and he very much believed in witchcraft," Benjamin says. "I had also started to believe in that kind of thinking and became very badly behaved."

When Benjamin's parents split up over his father's infidelity, the boy was relegated to a life on the street. "I used to fight almost everyone no matter their age, including even stoning people." Benjamin says. "I spent many nights sleeping on the streets. I had a big shirt that was beyond my size and I could fold my arms and legs into it so it would cover me up. I remember some nights I spent in the church and other nights on the side of the road."

Benjamin's mother eventually began operating a small shop next door to Bishop John Michael Mugerwa's veranda, a grocery business she had taken over from her brother who had gradually been driven insane by the challenges of life in Katwe. Kobugabe was constantly borrowing money from various people to keep the shop open without any clear idea about how she was going to pay it back. When Kobugabe started working at the grocery, she brought Benjamin and his younger sister Gloria to live with her. Some nights they slept in a small room behind the grocery stall and others in a nearby shack.

At one point, Katende, who was running his chess project next door, asked Kobugabe if he could store flour at her shop because it was being stolen from its previous location, and also to cook the daily porridge on her stoop. Kobugabe began noticing the enthusiastic children at the chess project and told Benjamin that he should join. Benjamin initially refused, convinced he wouldn't like chess, before he finally capitulated, like so many others, because it ensured him a meal every day.

It didn't take long for Ivan to realize that he was teaching a natural. Benjamin was the most instinctive chess player Ivan had met in the project. Benjamin's brain was wired for the game. Within months Benjamin was the best player in the program, eclipsing Ivan and the rest of the Pioneers. Benjamin could be beaten only by his own considerable hubris, which he'd developed over time to mask the pain of his childhood. Once after Benjamin lost a game against a clearly inferior opponent, Katende approached Benjamin and asked, "Do you know why you lost?"

"No," Benjamin said.

"You lost," Katende said, "because of too much pride."

"Because I had learned the game so easily I thought I knew everything about chess," Benjamin says. "I used to treat the other children in the project as if nobody else mattered. So I started changing my character and the other kids began seeing me as a model, began listening to me unlike before when no one even dared to be close to me because I was known as one of the notorious children in the slum."

Benjamin became an ambassador for the chess project, recruiting other kids to join, including his sister Gloria, Phiona's initial tutor. When Benjamin started teaching and practicing with Gloria, he found that it helped him understand the game even better.

In 2008, with debt collectors on her trail, Benjamin's mother suddenly disappeared. Benjamin heard through relatives that Kobugabe had gone to "the islands," some small shards of land that were part of Uganda's territory in Lake Victoria, an area known to be even more lawless than Katwe. Kobugabe said she was going to get a job there and then come back to repay her debts. Since then she has contacted Benjamin only once, saying she was leaving the country, again supposedly to find work. When Katende tried to speak to Benjamin's father, Wilson Mubiru, to ask him to be more responsible for Benjamin and his other children, Mubiru said he had remarried with three new children and that he was broke.

So Benjamin was left to take care of his two younger siblings, the three of them living in the room behind the grocery stall and Benjamin washing their clothes and cooking meals whenever food was available. "They greatly rely on me and I very much desire that I invest my life in them," says Benjamin, who believes he is 13 years old. "Luckily enough the sisters to my mother are not bad people. They try to support us as if we are their children. I don't know if I will ever see my mother again. You never know."

Benjamin says that Katende has taught him to seize any opportunity that is available and try not to be discouraged by his past. "The way that I grew up somehow trained me to be on my own," Benjamin says. "My younger brother does not even know who our mother is, but I very much believe that it really affects my young sister. Many times she even mentions it to me, 'I wish our mother was here.' When I am at home with them I feel somehow tormented, but I get courage and I say, 'No, if other people have been able to stand, can't I also stand?'"

Benjamin was the first boy ever to play chess with Phiona at the project. He normally didn't play against newcomers, who tended to segregate themselves in their own corner of the veranda, but he recognized that Phiona had initially trained with his sister, so he took an interest in her as well.

"The first time I played against Phiona I was surprised that she gave me some challenges and I thought she had a chance to be good with training," Benjamin says. "I told her, 'The big deal with chess is planning. What's the next move? How can you get out of the attack they have made against you?' We make decisions like that every day in the slum."

Says Ivan, "When Phiona first came I thought, 'What does she want here?' During those days we rarely played girls. When Phiona first arrived I took it for granted that girls are always weak, that girls can do nothing, but I came to realize that a girl can play good chess. Phiona wanted chess seriously. Her level of playing was like the level of boys. She played like a boy. She thought like a boy."

Ivan, several years older than Phiona, and Benjamin, several years her junior, would become Phiona's primary mentors in the project. Though the three played at different levels, they became bonded by a shared obsession with the game. With no other distractions and nowhere else to go, they would train together for hours and hours, day after day.

While other girls in the project were afraid to play against boys, Phiona relished it and her game matured quickly. "She was always saying that boys are very difficult to play, but she became used to that," Benjamin says. "It felt normal for her to play against boys and she wanted to play against boys because she thought that would make her a better player."

Phiona did not find it intimidating to play against boys because at home she was the only girl. During her early development in the game, influenced by her male opponents, she played too recklessly, attacking blindly without much thought to the consequences, just as she did in her neighborhood fights. She often sacrificed crucial pieces in risky attempts to capture pieces as quickly as possible, even when playing black—second in a chess game—which usually dictates a defensive posture in the opening.

"I learned that chess is a lot like my life," Phiona says. "If you make smart moves you can stay away from danger, but you know any bad decision could be your last. When I first started playing, I lost so many games before the boys convinced me to act more like a girl and play with calm and patience."

Phiona remembers almost nothing about the game, except the outcome. Joseph Asaba can recall every single move. It occurred sometime in 2006. Phiona had been at the chess project for several months. She isn't sure how many games she played and lost without ever winning, saying only that the number is too high to count.

Phiona was anxious as she sat down across the board from Joseph, who had specifically requested her as an opponent because he expected to beat her, and winners at the project are usually allowed to keep playing on a board until they are defeated. Phiona had played against Joseph a few times before and he had always won within a few moves.

How could he do that? It seemed like magic to her. It wasn't. It was the Fool's Mate.

Joseph had learned the Fool's Mate from Katende and it was his favorite tactic. He used it in every game he played. So again in this game against Phiona, Joseph employed his customary opening, maneuvering his bishop and queen into position. He thought the trap was set as usual. But this time Phiona responded by moving her queen directly in front of her king. Joseph had never seen that before, but he still jumped at the opportunity to capture Phiona's pawn with his queen. Phiona then took Joseph's queen and his bishop, while forfeiting her queen and a pawn, an advantageous swap.

"By the time I laid my usual plan, it seemed that there was someone who revealed my plot to her because she recognized how to defend it and guard her king," Joseph says. "I knew I could not win with the Fool's Mate because there was someone who revealed to her my tricks."

"Coach Robert taught me how to defend the Fool's Mate," Phiona says with a sly smile. "Coach told me to bring the queen in front of the king and I would take two pieces from him and then the game could play on."

After the Fool's Mate failed, Joseph didn't know what to do next. He was never comfortable in the middlegame because he rarely had to play it.

"I started advancing my pawns and I captured her bishop and she took my knight," Joseph remembers. "Then she forked my pieces and I had never seen that before. She put my two pieces in target and I knew she would capture one and I had to ask myself which one I should defend. So I played a back move to try to guard the rook, but when I tried to guard it, she still captured it. I can't forget that game."

The problem for Phiona was that without her queen, she didn't have any idea how to win a game with the other pieces. She didn't believe she could mate without the queen. So the two continued playing. Phiona had two rooks on the board, and she used them to protect an advancing pawn until she executed a queening. Once she recovered her queen, she used that to try to mate.

Because Phiona had never successfully checkmated an opponent, she didn't really know how to do it. She kept putting Joseph in check without a clear strategy to finish the game. "At the end, I remember I didn't know that I had won the game," Phiona says. "Joseph might have known, but he did not reveal it. The other children watching were saying, 'Phiona has won the game! Phiona has won the game!' I didn't know what they were talking about, so I just played the move I had already planned and it was the right move to mate him."

Suddenly Phiona realized that Joseph's king had nowhere safe to go. He had been arrested. That's when she realized that maybe the game was over.

One of the game's spectators, Wilson Mugwanya, said, "Eh, Joseph, you are not serious. A girl? A girl has mated you?"

Joseph slumped over the board and began to cry. Instead of celebrating, Phiona found herself consoling her first victim. Joseph told Phiona that he would never, ever, play her again.

"When she mated me, I felt so bad," Joseph says. "The person who all along I have been winning with the Fool's Mate and now she has won me? All along I teased her and I knew she was very weak and I felt very bad when I lost to her because I learned the game before her so I felt that a learner should not beat me. This was a person I used to teach. How can she now challenge me and be able to win?"

Phiona rarely left the project early, rarely left the place she felt most comfortable in her world before Katende kicked her out, but she didn't play any more games that day. She went straight home, five kilometers across Katwe at a giddy gallop to tell her mother that she had won a game of chess. And against a boy.

Harriet didn't understand chess. When she was told about the little pieces that looked like castles and animals moving around a board of different-colored squares, she assumed it was a child's game.

"At first when Phiona went to play chess with Brian, I didn't know what chess was and I didn't take it seriously," Harriet says. "I wasn't certain about what they were really doing there. She and Brian tried to explain the game to me, but my head was too weak."

All Harriet knew was that the chess program guaranteed her children a meal each day, which was more than she could do, so after initially resisting, and over Brian's repeated objections early on, Harriet began exempting Brian and Phiona from selling maize in the afternoons so they could play chess.

News eventually spread around Katwe that the chess project was part of an organization run by white people, known throughout much of Africa as *mzungu*.

One day Harriet had a disturbing conversation with some of the other mothers in her neighborhood who told her that they refused to let their children go to the project and warned her not to allow her children to attend.

"The neighbors said a lot that terrified me," Harriet says. "They told me that chess is the white man's game and if my kids go there and interact with them that the mzungu will steal them and never bring them back. But I could not afford to feed them. I had to trust the mzungu. What choice did I have?"

Chapter 6
Mzungu

Andrew Popp plays with children at a Chinese orphanage during
his school year abroad in 2003.

Mzungu is a Swahili word that translates as "someone who wanders around without purpose." The term was initially used by Africans to describe European missionaries and explorers, then later traders, colonists, and eventually tourists. The word *mzungu* has come to encompass all white people and is usually tinged with distrust born of years of exploitation by those who fit the description. However, without mzungu there would be no Coach Robert and without Coach Robert, Phiona Mutesi would likely still be selling maize from a saucepan on her head, assuming there was still a Phiona at all. While the mzungu in Phiona's story come from far away and have lived vastly different lives, the disparity in their journeys from those of Phiona and Robert Katende aren't as stark as they might initially appear. They are all wanderers, but none without a purpose.

Carl Russell Hammond, Jr. was born in suburban Boston on July 16, 1933, the son of an international banker. The Hammonds lived a cozy, upper-middle-class life in their white two-story colonial home until the day when the boy they called Russ was four years old and his life turned upside down. One evening, when his father, Carl, Sr., was away on a business trip, Russ's mother, Helen, told Russ and his older sister, Daphne, that they were moving to California where their grandmother lived. Helen didn't mention divorce. Russ didn't understand what was going on, but he didn't question his mother's authority. He just packed his belongings as she requested and boarded the train, unsure if he would ever see his father again.

Four days later, Helen and her two children arrived in California to a far less comfortable life. Russ and Daphne were taken in by their grandmother while Helen searched for work. It was the tail end of the Great Depression.

Shortly after the family arrived in California, Helen's mother moved to Bellflower, a hardscrabble suburb of Los Angeles, where for the next few months she and the two children lived in a small shack where they cooked over a wood stove and the kids bathed in a tin tub located in a storage shed behind the house.

At age five, Russ and his sister moved back to Los Angeles to live with their mother. A latchkey kid, Russ organized a bunch of local boys into a gang who used to hang out at the local Woolworth's and shoplift candy to fill their starving bellies. In 1940, Helen married C. Robert Carr, her children assumed their stepfather's last name, and the family moved to Santa Barbara, where they continued to struggle. "We were so poor that I remember making sandwiches day after day from the peanut butter that I could scrape off the lid," Russ says. "My clothes were threadbare and my shoes had holes in them." Russ's chores included caring for three dozen chickens penned up behind the garage and cleaning out the chicken coop. He wandered the neighborhood daily selling eggs.

Russ Carr was an ill-behaved child who often got into fights, until a coach at Harding Elementary School, Gordon Gray, began to develop Russ's athletic ability as a way to lure him off the streets. Progressing through grade school, Russ was named captain of every sport he tried, from baseball to football to basketball.

One summer during junior high, Russ was invited to participate in a program called Camp Conestoga that included an overnight camping trip. He and 14 other boys were bedded down for a night in the woods when sometime before dawn, Russ says he awoke to a bright light above him. He initially thought he was dreaming. "I heard a voice that I thought must be an angel speaking to me," Carr remembers. "The voice said, 'I have chosen you to follow me.' That moment began my spiritual journey."

During his senior year at Santa Barbara High School, Russ met Jay

Beaumont, a student at local Westmont College, who recruited him to join the Christian group Young Life. After high school, the St. Louis Browns offered Carr a chance to play professional baseball, but he opted to concentrate on his education and seek his spiritual direction, eventually choosing to follow Beaumont to Westmont College, where Russ would meet his future wife, Sue. Russ enrolled with ten cents in his pocket. His mother couldn't believe he'd turned down a professional baseball contract as well as athletic scholarships to the University of Arizona and UCLA.

Russ graduated from Westmont in 1956 with plans to become a teacher, and the Carrs began an odyssey that included four children and 18 moves over three decades. At each stop, Carr took a personal interest in the most troubled students. At one Oregon school he met a girl who wore the same stained, dirty dress every day. Carr drove to her home, which consisted of two rooms and an outhouse, with no electricity or running water. The mother had abandoned the family. The father worked as a logger, and the responsibility of raising her three younger siblings fell to the girl in Carr's class. To bathe she had to go to a nearby creek, then carry water back for drinking and cooking. After Carr discovered her circumstances, the girl was given a locker in the women's dressing room at school, which was stocked with toiletries, and a job in the cafeteria where she was able to eat a square meal each day.

The Carrs eventually moved to Washington, to Germany, and to England, before coming full circle back to Santa Barbara in 1966 when Carr accepted a job at Westmont College as a teacher as well as the school's baseball and soccer coach. Carr had never played soccer in school but had developed an interest in the sport during his three years living in Europe.

At the end of the 1968 baseball season, Carr was faced with a decision. Both soccer and baseball were year-round programs and each team felt neglected when Carr coached the other sport. Carr gave up baseball and decided to pour his full energy into his soccer program. "Later, I could look back and realize how God had a hand in my decision," Carr says. "Soccer would ultimately lead me into the next phase of my life and serve as the vehicle to open doors to what would become my true calling."

Who knows when the light bulb actually turned on? The passage of time has obscured exactly when the idea first struck him. But for Russ Carr it may have happened in a park in Guatemala. Carr traveled to Guatemala City in 1974 as the coach of a collegiate all-star soccer team on a Christian barnstorming tour through Central America. He and two of his players left their hotel one afternoon to kick around a soccer ball in a local park, and before long, 50 Guatemalan children showed up out of nowhere wanting to play. As Carr and the two players scrimmaged with the kids and tried to communicate across the language barrier, Carr began to view it as a seminal moment. At one point he stepped out of the game to soak in the joy on the children's faces. That steamy afternoon in Central America felt like a beginning. The seed of sports outreach to underdeveloped countries had been planted.

In 1982, Carr chose to leave his job and friends behind in Santa Barbara and move across the country to Lynchburg, Virginia, where he and Sue purchased a farmhouse flanked by two five-acre meadows. Carr planned to use those meadows for soccer fields, staging areas for his future sports ministry. Shortly after he arrived in Lynchburg, Carr accepted a job at Liberty University, the Christian school founded by Rev. Jerry Fallwell, where he eventually met Vernon Brewer, the director of Liberty's Light Ministry, a student mission group. In 1987 Brewer was preparing to take his annual summer mission trip with Liberty students when he approached Carr about joining the group as a basketball coach.

Carr agreed and then asked, "Where will the first stop be?"

Brewer replied, "Uganda."

During his visit to Uganda with the team, Carr and his six players staged basketball clinics at schools and organized a workout program for the Ugandan national basketball team. They also shared their testimony at churches, hospitals, and a prison, as well as in the streets of Kampala.

One afternoon a man who had been a student at Kampala University during the Idi Amin regime approached Carr and tearfully shared his story about returning home for lunch one day to find his father, mother, three brothers, and two sisters murdered by Amin's soldiers. Carr comforted the heartbroken man, who was inspired that day to convert to Christianity. At that moment, Carr decided to make a long-term commitment to do whatever he possibly could to fix what ailed Uganda.

By the time he and the Liberty team returned to Uganda the following year, Carr had officially founded Sports Outreach Institute. The organization's mission would be to use soccer as a catalyst to offer the guidance of religion to the country's most impoverished people. Uganda's National Council of Sports assigned a man named Barnabas Mwesiga to act as the group's host and guide. Mwesiga was one of the best strikers ever to play for the Ugandan national soccer team and also the team's former coach. Carr and Mwesiga struck up a friendship over their shared interest in soccer and coaching and Mwesiga would become the first Ugandan to accept a job with Sports Outreach.

"They discovered me and I see it as a blessing," Mwesiga says. "I didn't know about sports ministry. My interest all along was to raise young people to accept soccer as a means of improving their lives. Then when the ministry came in, I found an additional tool."

In 1995 Mwesiga introduced Carr to Aloysius Kyazze, the former Uganda national team captain. Carr immediately saw that Kyazze shared his passion and offered him a position with Sports Outreach as well. At the time, Kyazze was coaching a soccer team of born-again Christians called Miracle, grooming several young sports ministers including a gifted striker by the name of Robert Katende.

One morning probably in 2002, with Barnabas Mwesiga at the steering wheel driving down a dirt road in Southern Uganda toward another village where he and Carr would preach, the two began talking about the burgeoning numbers of slum youth in Kampala. Suddenly an idea flashed through Carr's mind. He began to outline a plan on his yellow notepad that would ultimately become the blueprint for Sports Outreach in the city slums.

Carr plotted the foundation of the plan with Mwesiga that day. Soccer players with leadership potential would be selected to form a team called the Good News Football Club and then would be trained in how to implement Carr's program for children in the slums. The projects would ultimately include five components: sports, vocational training, community service, education, and meals—all under an umbrella of discipleship—and would first be implemented in three of Kampala's eight slums: Kibuli, Nateete, and Katwe.

Understanding that mzungu such as him would initially be viewed either with suspicion or as a target for a bribe, Carr sought ways to gain the respect and acceptance of the slum communities. His team would first contact the local leader elected by the people of that slum district and gain approval for some community service that would include collecting trash and clearing out drainage ditches. After several hours of cleanup, they would bring out soccer balls and encourage children to participate in a variety of games.

Carr, who was nearly 70 by then, knew he was getting too old to spearhead his plan over the long term. He needed somebody who could take his vision and expand upon it. The Sports Outreach board asked Carr to find an American who would recruit the next generation of Ugandan leaders for the organization. One day Carr invited a local pastor named Rodney Suddith to visit his Virginia farm. During a tour of the grounds, Carr explained to Suddith his vision of sports ministry.

"Gosh, I guess I've kind of been working as a sports minister my whole life," Suddith told Carr in his syrupy Southern drawl. "I just never knew there was such a thing."

"I think I was raised in Camelot," Rodney Suddith says.

It was actually Newport News, Virginia, in the 1950s. Rodney's father, Joseph Buxton "Buck" Suddith, was a classic blue-collar World War II vet. Buck's father had been a timekeeper in the shipyard. Buck grew up by the water and loved sailing, and it was always understood he would follow his father to work in the shipyard as well. Buck finished high school and then joined the United States Merchant Marine in World War II. When he returned from the war, he married Lois Parker and they had four children, including Rodney, born in 1949.

Buck got a job as an electrician at the shipyard in Newport News and the Suddiths lived in a two-room bungalow on Gambol Street in a neighborhood called Green Oaks, not far from the docks. Every father in Green Oaks was a shipyard worker, the patron of a lower-middle-class family, and no one ever moved. Along Gambol Street the families had names like Ostrosky, Turnidge, Judkins, Smith, Pulley, Schaumberg, and Mackenzie. Their roots traced all over the world. They were all white.

"I was never in a classroom with a person of color all the way through high school, yet my parents taught me to be very sensitive to everyone," Suddith says. "We were never allowed to make any kind of negative statement about any ethnic group or person of color. It was a very segregated time in the South, so people all around us would, but never a Suddith. At the time I didn't understand what a powerful life lesson that was."

On Rodney's first day of first grade he and the other students were asked to count as high as they could. Some of the other kids had gone to preschool or kindergarten. Rodney had not, because no one in his neighborhood did. All of the other students in the class could print their names. Rodney didn't know how to write an *R*. Because he was sitting in the front row, Rodney was the first to stand up and count. He counted to six.

"I was six years old and I thought that was pretty good," Suddith says. "Well, right behind me there were kids counting to places I'd never heard of, counting beyond a hundred, and it was really kind of a humbling experience. I think that's when I began to realize there was a competitive streak in me. I felt embarrassed and I didn't want to be in that position again. I wanted to push myself a little bit more."

For most of his childhood Rodney did not own a bike. The yards along Gambol Street were small, so if the kids in the neighborhood wanted to play baseball, they needed to go to Deer Park, about two miles away. When the other kids pedaled off on their bikes for Deer Park, Rodney took off running on a shortcut through the woods and would usually be the first one to arrive. Those jogs developed in him an interest in running that blossomed as Rodney grew older. The sport clicked with him. Rodney was an introvert and running fit his personality.

Because he was not naturally fast, Rodney's track teammates at Warwick High School jokingly called him "Rocket." He eventually found his niche as a miler, thriving on guts and determination, driven by a visceral fear of losing to other runners that he knew possessed more talent.

"High school sports taught me what it is to live in-between," Suddith says. "I think that's the greatest lesson I ever learned from sports. Mentally most of us are in between where we would like to be and where we are. I had an idea what I wanted and I wasn't there yet, but I really wanted to get there. If I decided that I wanted to reach a certain level in a classroom or on the field then before I could achieve it, I would always raise the standard a little bit higher."

During many of his races in high school, Rodney would push himself well beyond his comfort zone and after the race he would urinate blood. The harder he ran, the more blood. "I knew my body was failing," Suddith says. "But in the neighborhood I grew up in, if you had a problem like that, you kept it to yourself."

When Rodney was a junior in high school, he was called to the guidance office where his counselor said, "We'd like you to start looking at colleges."

"College?" Rodney said. "I'm going to work in the shipyard."

"But you can go to William & Mary on a scholarship."

Rodney spent the rest of the day thinking for the first time about attending college, about leaving the predestined path of his life. That night Rodney discussed the idea with his father, who was clearly disappointed. Buck's circle believed that when you finished high school, you went to work. He spoke derisively about "college boys." Then Buck said, "Do you think you're too good for the shipyard?"

"No, I don't think that at all," Rodney said. "I just think there might be something else out there."

At William & Mary in the late 1960s there were still very few people of color in Rodney Suddith's class. Like so many college students at that time, he was trying to figure out the rapidly changing rules in American society. So he decided to spend a semester at Hampton University, leaving a campus that was nearly all white for a campus almost entirely black.

"I wasn't embraced for being different and that was really an eye-opener for me," Suddith says of Hampton. "I learned more about myself because although I'm an introvert by nature, I didn't really like being totally alone, feeling isolated just based on my appearance, especially when I didn't know how to cross that barrier to feel comfortable."

As an athlete at William & Mary, Suddith found himself firmly in-between. His team included two sub-4-minute milers. That was always Suddith's goal, breaking four minutes. In one dual meet in his sophomore year he was on pace to finally achieve it when, during a rough race, he was knocked off stride in the final turn and finished third in a time of 4:00.3. Suddith would never get that close again.

After his sophomore year, Suddith qualified for the 1972 Olympic Trials in the mile. As a 23-year-old, he figured those Olympics in Munich would likely be his only chance to run on that grand stage. When Suddith arrived at the trials in Eugene, Oregon, he found out just how small his pond was. He was intimidated and his body was failing him. He didn't make it past the first heat.

"That's when my kidney really started getting bad and I could tell I was coming undone," Suddith says. "That was the era when they were just starting to check pee and when they got a cup of my pee, I knew my running career was over."

Suddith underwent surgery that evening and doctors discovered he suffered from a birth defect. One of his kidneys had deteriorated to the point of failure. Competitive running was putting too much pressure on his renal system and the kidney had to be removed. Says Suddith, "I was haunted by the idea that I knew I'd never have another chance to chase my athletic dreams."

Suddith would become the first in his family ever to graduate from college. He then went to graduate school at Virginia Commonwealth University, where he earned a teacher's certificate and met his future wife, Janice. Suddith's first teaching job was at Thomas Jefferson High School, an inner-city school in Richmond. The student population consisted almost entirely of black students bused into a mostly white neighborhood. Suddith taught history and political science and became an assistant coach for the track team, which captured four state championships over the next seven years. "In some ways it was the most rewarding place to be because you were really giving people hands up," Suddith says. "I remember seeing kids graduate and go to Harvard, but I found out that most stories in the inner-city don't end as you'd like."

Suddith was particularly affected by the story of Sherrie Trent, one of the female runners on Jefferson High's team. Suddith used to drive his orange Volkswagen beetle into the projects each morning at 5 A.M. to pick up Sherrie for what was known as Dawn Patrol, the team's early-morning workouts. "One night I got a call that Sherrie's mother and a boyfriend had been in an argument and that he'd just killed Sherrie with a shotgun right in front of her mother," Suddith says. "Going through that, I realized there are some things I can't control and that are beyond my comprehension. That just wore me down."

Sherrie's death helped trigger the end of Suddith's tenure at Jefferson High. On the day Sherrie's teammates won the state championship in her honor, Suddith received a job offer to teach and coach at E. C. Glass High School in Lynchburg. Suddith knew he needed a change. He took the job.

Suddith ended up coaching at Glass High for only a short time; at the end of one track season, he promptly quit. Suddith had a strong spiritual sense that he was supposed to be doing something else. He and Janice had four children and Suddith had become deeply involved in his church. Eventually the church asked him if he would do full-time service as the director of Christian education. Suddith had no real training other than his parents being Sunday school teachers and some knowledge of the Bible, but he accepted the job despite his fear that he might be underqualified.

The same year Suddith arrived in Lynchburg, Russ Carr bought his farm as a staging area for his new path in life. One of the elders at Suddith's church had helped Carr buy his property and suggested to Suddith that he meet Carr. Suddith asked why. "Remember when you told us we should use sports to help kids in the church?" the elder said. "Well, Russ is talking about that weird stuff, too. We don't get it, but you all might bond."

Eight years later, Rodney Suddith stood beside Russ Carr in Gulu, Uganda. Gulu was then Uganda's headquarters for horror. Thousands of children were being kidnapped by Joseph Kony and his vicious cadre of rebels known as the Lord's Resistance Army. Those children were either killed or forced to become child soldiers in the LRA. Suddith and Carr stared in amazement on their first night in Gulu as thousands of children, some as young as three years old and carrying only a blanket, walked from the surrounding villages into Gulu's many camps for internally displaced people, hoping to escape the LRA. Aloysius Kyazze, who directed Sports Outreach's operation in Gulu, told them these kids were known as "night commuters" or "the invisible children."

Kyazze shared stories about children who had been forced by the rebels to kill their parents as they were being abducted. Young girls were repeatedly raped and tortured while others were sold as slaves. When these children escaped the LRA or were liberated by government troops, their emotional state was in complete collapse. As Suddith surveyed this scene and listened to stories from survivors, he sensed his life was about to change again.

"It was horrific seeing thousands of kids in a fenced area just trying to feel safe because they were afraid they were going to be kidnapped or murdered," Suddith says. "I looked at my life and it was such a disconnect. I'd become so isolated and so secure that I was as boring as dirty water. I had gotten away from the in-between. When I got home from Uganda I talked to my wife and in an unfair way I used the ultimate Christian phrase on her: *I think God's calling me to this.*"

Suddith experienced a similar gut reaction the first time he visited Katwe. "I'd been to some pretty tough places on mission trips, but the face of hopelessness is a scary one to me because often times those faces turn to violence, either against themselves or against others," Suddith says. "My first experience in the Katwe slum was looking at a powder keg about to explode. Outsiders would tell me that the people there need Jesus. I would say, 'Yes, they do, but they also need education, they need job training, they need food.'"

Suddith realized that Uganda, like most developing countries, did not provide the same economic safety net for its poorest people that exists in America and he thought Sports Outreach should attempt to fill some of that void. Rather than take a purely evangelical approach, Suddith began with Carr's blueprint and devised his own holistic approach, leaning on six tenets: social, psychological, emotional, mental, physical, and spiritual.

"I thought there was no way to address this problem solely on a purely spiritual level," Suddith says. "We can't just tell these children, 'Don't fear, God is with you.' We've got to show them we can address all of their challenges. I would go to the slums and see where a Christian organization had come in and converted hundreds of people, but that didn't stick. Others fed people, but if that's all you do, then who's going to feed them tomorrow?"

Carr's mandate to Suddith was to help develop the young leaders mentored by Mwesiga and Kyazze. The first time Suddith met Robert Katende he immediately recognized his potential.

"There was something special about Robert, a certain dignity and awareness that just stood out," Suddith says. "Robert would have scared me if I had to compete against him. He had just begun the chess program and what amazed me about it was that he had a grand plan. The plan wasn't just that this was an alternative activity for the kids who don't want to play soccer. The plan was that these kids are going to learn from him, they're going to get better in school, become more socially interactive, become young people with a chance to succeed."

When some of the purists in the Sports Outreach community complained that chess wasn't really a sport and shouldn't take any time away from soccer, Suddith was there to back Katende. Suddith, who has shuttled between Virginia and Uganda dozens of times over the past decade, has become a valued mentor for Katende and the other two dozen young Ugandan Sports Outreach ministers.

"My goal is to help these poor children grow and to do that I try to train Robert and the other leaders how to stay in-between," Suddith says. "If someday I went to Uganda and met the ministers and children that I'm blessed to work with and I thought that this was all that they would ever be, it would really crush me. People who know me best say that if there's any good quality I have, it is a way of helping people get from where they are to where they want to be. I believe I am called to help others who are not able to count past six, but really, really want to get to seven."

Santa Barbara, California, is one of the best places on earth. In many ways, it really is Camelot. It is beautiful, prosperous, and nurturing of children—everything Katwe is not. Andrew Popp grew up there.

Andrew's parents, Norm and Tricia, describe their only son as kind and thoughtful and sensitive and impressionable. As a young boy, Andrew loved to read. Possessed with a vivid imagination, Andrew would lose himself in stories. Once, after reading *Aladdin,* he had nightmares for a week about the villain Jafar. Andrew was a very driven child, who learned how to play guitar, piano, and drums. As a fourth grader he was asked to choose a younger child to counsel for his school's Big Buddy program. All of the other kids shied away from one particular child with Down syndrome. Andrew said that was the only kid he wanted to mentor. As a sixth grader during reading period, while the rest of the kids flipped through comic books or teen magazines, Andrew read the Bible.

Andrew was a dreamer. He grew up wanting to drive monster trucks and then he wanted to be a professional surfer and then he wanted to be seven feet tall, until he discovered girls and realized that his 6'9" stature was plenty tall enough. His proud parents describe him as larger than life.

Andrew Popp was another person for whom sports had the potential to change his life. He and his father would play basketball for hours on their driveway hoop and Norm coached his son in the sport until high school. During Andrew's junior year at San Marcos High School, he studied in China, learning the language and playing on a basketball team there. He also taught the game to children while on a church mission to Guatemala during the following summer of 2004.

As a senior at San Marcos High, Andrew earned all-league honors in both volleyball as a middle blocker and basketball as his team's starting center. He also scored over 1500 on the SATs, which made him a model student-athlete for college recruiters. He could have his choice of college. Andrew was recruited by dozens of schools around the country for basketball, but his dream was always to attend an Ivy League school like Harvard or Yale. Those schools showed interest in him, but for reasons that his parents still cannot explain, Andrew began to unravel psychologically during his senior year and when it came time to submit his college applications, Andrew missed the deadlines and those schools eventually lost interest.

In 2005—the same year that half a world away nine-year-old Phiona Mutesi first sat down at a chessboard and began to change her life—very early one summer morning just weeks after his high school graduation, 18-year-old Andrew Popp drove along San Marcos Pass Road up into the mountains to Cold Spring Canyon Bridge, a 1,200-foot-long steel arch along California State Route 154 that spans a valley connecting Santa Barbara to Santa Ynez. At about 5:15 A.M. a deputy sheriff driving to work spotted Andrew's car on fire at the bridge's north end and Andrew inching his way from the centerline of the bridge toward the thigh-high guardrail. When the policeman approached, Andrew, with a blank stare on his face, leaped backward and dropped 200 feet into a foggy wooded ravine.

Norm and Tricia Popp were devastated. They initially struggled with how to memorialize their son. Then they recalled one Sunday morning at Santa Barbara Community Church, when their family heard an evangelist named Russ Carr speak so passionately about his vision for Sports Outreach Institute. The Popps decided the organization's focus on children, sports, and academics perfectly reflected who Andrew was. Instead of flowers, the Popps requested that donations be sent to Sports Outreach in their son's name. When the Popps realized the potential of that money to help dozens of children in Uganda pay for school, they took the funds they had planned to spend on Andrew's college education and with Suddith's help they created the Andrew Popp Memorial Scholarship.

For years after his death, Andrew's parents could never bring themselves to witness the fruits of the scholarship. Suddith kept encouraging them to come to Uganda and on the five-year anniversary of their son's suicide, the Popps traveled to Kampala and met Phiona Mutesi and the 60 other slum children who would not be attending school were it not for the Andrew Popp Memorial Scholarship. It sounds like a simple story of redemption, but for the Popps, it is far more complicated than that.

Standing on the balcony at the Namirembe Guest House in Kampala, on the morning of September 18, 2010, Andrew's parents spoke about what visiting the children studying on the Popp Scholarship meant to them:

Tricia Popp: "Coming to Uganda has crystallized my understanding of our experience. As a Westerner we don't like to face death and we don't like to face loss. We had difficulty navigating that experience because it was so foreign to us. Our life has been completely upended and so this experience has been amazing for me. Phiona's life brings us such joy. It's an incredible gift. I will never lose the sadness of losing Andrew and we would want him back in a heartbeat, but I'm so grateful to be able to celebrate Phiona's life. I think what I've learned is that's why we have two hands. There's life and there's death. This trip has helped me understand death and life and their interconnection.

"I think people want us to be who we were, but I don't want to ever be the same. I want to embrace Andrew's loss just as Phiona has had to embrace all the hardship in her life. I feel so much more a sense of wholeness despite my loss because this trip helps me understand that most of the world suffers so much more than we do. To infuse Phiona's life with some hope is a huge gift. Phiona's mom thanked us. Are you kidding me? I thanked her for having the courage to face every day taking care of Phiona. We're both moms. I have sadness in my life as a mom and she does, too. I felt such solidarity with her. I feel like we're partners. I'm in no way helping her any more than she's helping me. When Phiona's mom knelt and said, 'Thank you,' I had this overwhelming clarity that we were all part of the same family and who wouldn't do what they could to help their family?

"Our son listened to some dark voice that said that his life was better off ended. That's too bad. He was my sweet boy. That's the mystery that we hold. It's a puzzle we'll never resolve and I don't think we're made to make sense of it. We spent two years asking why and we finally realized that you ask why until you can live with the why. This is helping us live with the why."

Norm Popp: "I don't know if I've ever tried to verbalize this before, but no matter how sick someone is or whatever their circumstances are, while they are still living there's hope. For me and my wife, dealing with the fact that Andrew was gone and there was no hope has been one of the hardest things to come to grips with. On this trip there are sixty-one kids on Popp Scholarship and we hope to see every one of them. There's no question their circumstances are dire. It's gut-wrenching. But at least there is hope there.

"One thing that's tricky is that people like to put a ribbon on tragedy. People say that there must have been a reason that Andrew died. There's no way in my mind that I will ever think that the good things that have come out of this were worth his death. Nothing could ever be worth that. Nothing can replace him. It's not a mathematical equation. It's not one for sixty-one. It doesn't add up that way. But it is redemptive in another way, because had that not happened we wouldn't be here. We wouldn't have started this scholarship. We, in a unique way, appreciate life and what it means the way kids don't.

"The connection we feel with Phiona is not like we've given this kid some money and she's doing well. We're pulling for her life in a way that she wouldn't understand, in a much deeper way. It's so tricky because Andrew didn't value life, because he didn't have any kind of perspective. I know these kids don't either, but if we can somehow help get them through and keep them alive, they might have hope for a future.

"I think that one of the difficult things is that we can't make a hero out of Andrew and yet we love him as much as any parent could. What he did wasn't in any way exemplary or a courageous thing. It was an impulsive thing in dealing with his problems. That's the rub. But we did want to honor him. He made a mistake that was permanent. Fortunately, most people make mistakes that are redeemable. As long as you're still alive there's no reason not to have hope and we are trying to communicate that to the kids that we see here. We aren't able to talk about the circumstances of Andrew's death particularly, but we are able to say, 'Hey, we lost our son and the life that he doesn't have, we'd like you to have. We'd like to have you alive with hope.'"

Phiona's annual school tuition, funded by the Andrew Popp Memorial Scholarship, is $75.

Middlegame

Chapter 7
Like a Boy, But Not a Boy

Robert Katende at the chessboard in Katwe with
Phiona Mutesi, the girl whom he believed he
could teach to become a "prophet" and eventually
a national champion.

C hess is generally believed to have originated in India sometime around the sixth century, where it was known by the Sanskrit name *chaturanga* and consisted of pieces divided into four divisions: infantry, cavalry, elephants, and chariotry. The game migrated through Persia, where it assumed the name *Shah Mat*, which translates to "the king is helpless" and is the origin of the English word "checkmate." The game then spread across Russia, where it would eventually be favored by the tsars, and into Western Europe, often transported to new regions by invading armies.

The pieces were named for roles in the courts of kings during the Middle Ages and play was modeled after how wars were contested in that period. In the 15th century the name *chess* first came into use and the game assumed the same general rules that have governed it ever since, with the queen as the most powerful piece on the board. By the early 1800s chess clubs and chess literature began to appear. In America, Thomas Jefferson and Benjamin Franklin both wrote about playing chess. The first modern chess tournament was staged in London in 1851. A few decades later, a Czech named Wilhelm Steinitz revolutionized the game by emphasizing the position of his pieces on the board to build strength and attack an opponent's weaknesses, utilizing his more theoretical approach to capture the first World Chess Championship in 1886.

Steinitz lost his title in 1894 to German mathematician Emanuel Lasker, who remained the world champion for a record 27 years. The epicenter of chess would gradually shift to the Soviet Union, where from 1948 until 2000 the world championship never left Russian hands, except between 1972 and 1975, when it was held by American Bobby Fischer. The International Olympic Committee officially recognized chess as a sport in 1999, but has yet to include it as part of the Olympic program because it lacks physical activity.

The highest ranking a player can achieve in chess is Grandmaster, a distinction earned primarily through consistently excellent play in events sanctioned by FIDE. In 1950 FIDE first awarded the title of Grandmaster to 27 players and there are now more than 1,300 male Grandmasters across the globe. Chess long being the provenance of men, very few women have ever broken into the top 500 rated players in the sport and it wasn't until 1991 that Susan Polgar became the first woman to earn a Grandmaster title on the same basis as her male counterparts. Polgar is currently among the 22 women who hold that title. There is also a gender-specific title, Woman Grandmaster, with lesser requirements, which has been achieved by more than 200 players.

Among the most popular sports in the world, chess infiltrated almost everywhere else on earth before it discovered sub-Saharan Africa. It needed 1,500 years to find Uganda. Initially introduced in Uganda through the country's colonial ties, chess was played only in homes and a few schools and clubs before the early 1970s. In 1972 a group of Ugandan doctors, inspired by the highly publicized world championship match between Fischer and Russian Boris Spassky, formed the Chess Association of Uganda. The group organized sporadic games in Kampala, often at Mulago Hospital or Makerere University, and would later become known as the Uganda Chess Federation after its affiliation with FIDE in 1976.

The first chess literature shared by the federation's players was a photocopied chess book given to Mathew Kibuuka, one of Uganda's trailblazers in the sport, as a wedding present. In the late 1970s the federation began publishing a small pamphlet called *Checkmate* that helped spread interest in the game. Uganda's chess evolution was further accelerated by an American chess administrator, Jerry Bibuld, who traveled to Uganda for a chess seminar in the early 1980s and subsequently began mailing issues of the United States Chess Federation magazine, *Chess Life*, to the Ugandan federation. "Reading *Chess Life* is how we learned the game," says current Ugandan national chess team coach Joachim Okoth, another of his nation's pioneers in the sport. "Before that we had read a few chess books and memorized some moves, but we didn't always know why we were making those moves. With Jerry's help, we learned why."

Of the 158 chess federations recognized by FIDE, Uganda's is among the most recently established. The first Ugandan national champion was an Englishman, a professor at Mbarara University. While Uganda has occasionally produced a strong player—the most notable is Willy Zabasajja, who won the Ugandan national championship a record nine times and became the first East African to earn the title of FIDE Master—the nation has never been ranked among the top 100 in the world in the FIDE ratings. While there are six Grandmasters in Africa, Uganda has never produced a Grandmaster or even an International Master, the level below Grandmaster and above FIDE Master. Because there is no translation for the word "chess" in her native Luganda language, whenever Phiona Mutesi talks about the game, she must shift into English for any chess terminology.

The man who first brought chess into Ugandan schools was Damien Grimes, a white Catholic priest and missionary who in 1967 took over as headmaster at Namasagali College, one of the most prestigious middle and high schools in the country at that time. Grimes began a chess program at Namasagali that slowly spread to other schools. Eventually Father Grimes organized a chess tournament among a few schools in Kampala, many of which also had headmasters from Great Britain. That tournament has since expanded to schools across the nation and adopted his name.

It was on the 2005 Father Grimes tournament where Robert Katende set his sights. His chess project had been in existence for a little over a year and the coach was beginning to sense that his players needed a goal. "I was concerned that what we were doing had started to become monotonous," Katende says. "You come one day. You train. You go. You come the next day. You train. You go. The question became, after that, what? I thought we needed to be training to go somewhere."

So Katende appealed to the chairman of the Uganda Chess Federation at the time, Enoch Barumba, requesting to enter players from his chess project in the 2005 Father Grimes tournament. The idea was emphatically rejected.

"Barumba was asking me, 'How can they come?'" Katende says. "He told me, 'These are street children. They do not go to school. How can they play in a schools tournament? How can they come and play students from well-established families? This cannot be allowed.' When I talked of slum children he thought he knew who they are. He thought they were dirty. He thought they were badly behaved. He thought they were hooligans who will offend the other children in some way. So he had all the reasons to refuse me."

Katende knew he would have to dispel a long-standing class prejudice in Uganda. Many Ugandans consider street children irredeemable and resist their integration into more privileged society. Katende visited Barumba numerous times over a period of three months, offering various ideas for how his program's children could compete in the tournament. He suggested that his players could compete as guest participants. He told Barumba that his children were young and inexperienced and certainly would not win a trophy, but they needed a platform to learn more about competitive chess. Katende also appealed to Godfrey Gali, the federation's general secretary.

"Robert's request was politically sensitive," Gali says. "When I spoke to the chairman he asked me, 'How do they fit in here?' He didn't want to allow that kind of arrangement, but I had met some of these kids and I convinced the chairman that we need to show that one of our federation's objectives is to spread the game to the entire Ugandan society."

Barumba finally relented, but under a condition that he suspected would preclude the slum kids from playing. "The registration cost was high and he knew I didn't have the money, so he said we could play as guest participants if we paid the registration," Katende says. "It was like a hurdle that he believed would rule us out. So I talked to Sports Outreach and they released the money and then I went back to Barumba and he was surprised that I had the money, but he had no way of taking back his words."

When Katende explained to the Pioneers what had happened, they could not believe it. "Before that time children had been dropping out of the program because they thought that chess was a waste of time," Ivan Mutesasira says. "Many had actually lost hope because they didn't see any future in playing chess, but when Coach Robert told us we were going for a tournament we were all surprised and excited."

Katende's team included the Pioneers: Samuel, Richard, Ivan, Julius, and Gerald, along with Phiona's brother Brian. The boys ranged in age from seven to 13 years old. For most of them, the 2005 Father Grimes tournament at King's College Budo in Mpigi was their first-ever trip out of the Katwe slum. When they were picked up in a van for the ride to King's College, it was their first time in a vehicle. During the 45-minute drive out of Kampala to Mpigi, Katende briefed the children on basic life skills, like how to open a water bottle and how to eat with silverware. They arrived to a vast campus full of trees and walkways threading through landscaped flowers. The playing hall was an austere theater with ceiling fans and glassed windows, neither of which the children had seen before. After letting the children soak in this new environment, Katende had a message for them. "It is us who know who we are," Katende told them. "They don't know who we are. What we need to do is to behave as if we live their life."

Katende tried to anticipate anything that could reveal the children's sheltered background, but some things were beyond his control. His players did not own any clothes that were not stained or torn. They were competing against children dressed in pressed school uniforms. Some even wore blazers and knickers.

"At the tournament we were isolated, and some of the other competitors laughed at our team and thought we were dirty, when in fact my players were wearing their best clothes and looking as smart as they could," Katende says. "Some of the students asked, 'Which school is this one?' Because it was their first time to see kids in this state."

Eventually, word leaked out that Katende's players were not schoolchildren at all. "They called us street kids," Ivan says. "We heard them say, 'Street kids? How do we play with street kids?' It was that kind of intimidation and torture. We were being shunned. They looked down on us."

When the tournament began, Katende's players were clearly affected by their treatment from the other players. They were all extremely nervous. "Gerald was shaking, the whole of himself shaking, so he could not even hold a piece," Katende says. "I told him, 'The people you are playing are not shaking. Just be confident. Don't mind if you lose. Just play as if we are still down there in Katwe training.'"

"Before the playing I would really feel good just to be in a new place I had never been," Samuel Mayanja says. "But as you go to play the game then you somehow develop some fear and many times I used to shiver at the board. Then I would remember coach telling me to be confident enough not to shiver. I could somehow gain some confidence. I could look at some of my other friends from the project and see them all stable and somehow playing very well and seated comfortably, so I somehow also developed that courage and started feeling better and better."

The tournament lasted for a week and Katende never let his players out of his sight. He was anxious about allowing them to interact with the other children because his players did not speak English well and he knew that could potentially lead to teasing and fights. While the students slept in dormitory beds, Katende and his children all slept on the dormitory floor sharing one mattress as a pillow. The kids from Katwe ate all of their meals together, marveling at their access to eggs, milk, bread, fruit, and the routine of three meals a day. "My kids would tell me, 'Coach, I am already satisfied and they are calling us for dinner,'" Katende says. "So they had to go for dinner with no room left in their stomachs. It was really something very exciting for them."

Katende's team finished the tournament ranked in the middle of the pack overall. They had outperformed many more-established chess programs, to the surprise of their coach. The certificate they received at the end of the tournament referred to them as "The Children's Team." They were given a tiny trophy and medals acknowledging them as the youngest team in the tournament.

"We sneaked the kids from the slum in there and fortunately they played well and they were very disciplined, even more disciplined than those who were formally in schools," Gali says. "When you asked them to assist with something, they rushed very fast to do it. In a way they touched my heart. They became darlings to us in the federation. Eventually even the other students realized that those kids were good, that they had potential, and they were eventually accepted."

While The Children's Team won some games at the 2005 Father Grimes Tournament, the lasting memory for Katende occurred when Ivan was playing a game in which he had a significant positional advantage and appeared certain to mate his opponent. Instead, Ivan committed a foolish blunder that forced him to settle for a draw.

"Ivan was sure that he would win and when it resulted in a draw he cried seriously, crying so loud that I had to get him out of the playing hall," Katende says. "The attitude from the school players was that this was an insult because this little kid is crying after he makes a draw against an older kid. I heard some people say, 'These street kids are funny. How do you cry over a game?' Those people didn't understand what the game meant to these children."

Because she had no other choice, Harriet let her children go.

Brian and Phiona returned to the dusty veranda each day to play chess. Occasionally, they could even borrow a board from Katende and return to their shack to play at home, game after game after game, neither sibling wanting to leave the board having lost the last game to the other, so they would play on until the last drops of kerosene burned out in their lamp.

"I remember the first time Phiona defeated me," Brian says. "We were all training for a tournament and we were paired together and Phiona won me. I felt ashamed, so what Phiona did is she told everybody that I was the one who won instead. That is a good sister. Ever since that day whenever she beats me, she isn't happy. She tells me the mistakes I made so that I can fix them and try to beat her the next time. She doesn't like beating me."

The truth is that Brian doesn't beat Phiona very much anymore, due in part to the time he has invested in making her a better player. "Coach Robert once told us that because there are so few girls playing chess in Uganda that Phiona had a chance to rise quickly in the game in our nation," Brian says. "So the boys at the project began to take more of an interest in seeing how good we can make her. Benjamin, Ivan, Samuel, we all want to put ourselves in her and see how far she can go."

By the time Phiona had learned the game, the barriers had been breached, the trail to chess tournaments in the outside world had been blazed by the Pioneers. They shared their incredible story upon returning from their first Father Grimes tournament and word got out as it does in Katwe. Before long, attendance at the chess project tripled.

With the teaching assistance of the kids he'd mentored in Katwe, Katende gradually expanded his chess project to three other slums: Kibuli, Nateete, and Bwaise. Katende often visited two or three of the slum projects on the same day. Knowing that in the future he wanted his kids to be more battle tested for tournaments like the Father Grimes event, Katende created his own competition contested among his four slum programs and called it the "interproject tournament."

Katende's first interproject tournament was staged in August of 2006 in the dining hall at the Kampala School for the Physically Handicapped, which shares its compound with the main office of Sports Outreach Institute. Katende had borrowed a sack of wooden chess pieces from the Uganda Chess Federation that were carved so crudely that it was difficult to tell a rook from a bishop. The chessboards were drawn onto pieces of cardboard, the squares carefully constructed with rulers and pens. Each morning Katende drove to his four chess projects in the slums to pick up the competitors and transport them to the site where they would play a game, then take a lunch break, then play more games in the afternoon before Katende delivered them all back to the slums each evening. The tournament lasted for three days.

Katende paid Samuel Mayanja's grandmother 15,000 shillings (about $8) for the event's grand prize: a duck. Richard Tugume, one of the Pioneers, won the duck, and other high finishers received 10,000 shillings. For the rest of the competitors, Katende raided a box of used T-shirts donated by mzungu. On the back of each he silk-screened S.O.I. CHESS ACADEMY. In future years, Katende would track down a "champion's trophy" from a donation box. Over the brass plate previously engraved with 1973 MOST IMPROVED PLAYER, Katende would glue a piece of paper on which he had written: INTERPROJECT CHESS TOURNAMENT CHAMPION. Nobody seemed to care that on top there was a baseball player catching a fly ball.

Barely noticed during that first interproject tournament was one shy and frightened girl competing in her first-ever tournament against a roomful of boys. Before her first game, Phiona stared around at the other tables and when she noticed she was the only girl among the two dozen players, she wondered if her being there was a mistake. She thought about asking Katende if she should simply watch the others play, but she was curious enough about what it would feel like to compete against all of these boys that she kept her seat and suppressed her anxiety.

"That day they told me we were going to play a tournament, I didn't even know what a tournament means," Phiona recalls. "For sure, I felt like I had some fear in me because I knew there were going to be other players from other places. I remember that first day I only won one game out of three, but it was in the last round. I somehow felt better and I thought, 'Tomorrow I'm coming back to challenge these people.'"

Phiona turned up the following day and won all three of her games, which qualified her to play some of the best players in the tournament on the final day. She lost both of her games that last day but no longer felt intimidated the way she had been just two days earlier. At the end of the tournament, Katende handed Phiona an envelope containing 15,000 shillings for winning the "girls' championship." Phiona could not believe she had earned it by playing chess. She brought the money home to her mother.

"What really motivated me greatly was that they gave me that gift," Phiona says. "They didn't give me a gift because I had won. They gave me a gift because I was the only girl who had taken part in the tournament, but that greatly motivated me to continue to play chess."

In January of 2007, just five months after her initial tournament experience at the interproject event, Phiona entered Uganda's Under-20 national championship held at the Lugogo Sports Complex. The tournament was well organized with real chessboards and pieces, as well as clocks to time the moves. Phiona was one of 20 participants from Katende's chess project entered into a tournament field of 70. Phiona was just 11 years old. Most of her opponents were 18 or 19.

Katende didn't watch Phiona play a single game in that tournament. With 20 children to follow, he concentrated most of his time on Ivan, Benjamin, Richard, and Gerald, four boys he thought might have a chance to win. But Phiona did capture the attention of Godfrey Gali, the Uganda Chess Federation's general secretary. Gali was initially intrigued by the sight of tiny Phiona with her unkempt hair, torn skirt, and flip-flops playing a well-dressed university student twice her size. He assumed the game would be a mismatch, but the longer he watched, the more Gali became captivated by the little girl's chess ability. "I remember when the game was near the end and Phiona was walking in a minefield," Gali says. "The only safe move to avoid losing the game was her knight to a specific space and she made that move. Now I was really interested. The next time her only safe move was her bishop to one particular place and I thought she would never see that move. She made that move. She made four successive moves when any other move would have finished her and she slowly turned the game until she'd won. At that point, I knew this girl had some potential to be a champion."

Because it was a round-robin format that mixed the boys and the girls, it was difficult to track the overall standings during the tournament. As the final results were tabulated, Phiona knew she had played well, but she never even considered the possibility that she might have won. Phiona waited anxiously as the names of the top female finishers were called. The winner was revealed last. That's when Phiona finally heard her name. She was the women's champion.

"It actually kind of blew my mind," Katende says. "Phiona had been playing only one year and she emerged the best girl against girls from well-established families. That's the first time I realized Phiona might be having something special."

Phiona won a gold trophy that stood almost as tall as she did. She had never held a trophy before, never really won anything in which there were other competitors.

"That was a very, very happy day," Phiona says. "I remember by the time I got home I felt like I was not the Phiona of always. I was a different Phiona."

In 2005 Robert Katende attended a chess tournament in Kampala with Godfrey Gali and as they watched a girl named Christine Namaganda win the championship, Katende shook his head incredulously. At that time, Christine dominated the girls' division in all of the local tournaments, but Katende believed that Christine's skills were not extraordinary. He turned to Gali and said, "Give me three years and I will develop someone who can be the girls' champion."

Katende thought that girl would be Farida Nankubuge, but Farida soon dropped out of the Katwe chess project when her parents found out that their Muslim daughter was playing with a Christian organization. They ordered her to sell sugarcane on the street during the time she had been playing chess.

So Katende focused on Phiona instead. And somewhat to his amazement, it had taken him only two years to produce a champion.

Katende took an even more intense interest in developing Phiona's game after she won the 2007 national junior championship. He admired her courage. He admired her drive. He admired how she walked five kilometers to get to the project each day when she first started and how when her family had to move even farther away from the veranda, Phiona just kept walking. All of this was unique to any girl he'd ever met in the program. Phiona was like a boy, but because she was not a boy, her opportunity to advance quickly in the game was mind-boggling.

Phiona had never read a chess book. Never read a chess magazine. Never used a computer. Yet this girl was already a national champion.

Katende told Phiona she would be a prophet. He told her about the inept doctor and the injections and asked, "If you don't believe in yourself, how do you expect anyone else to believe in you?" He told her how he learned chess and challenged her to be clever enough to keep growing in the game. He told her chess was a sport played by masters that was impossible to master, and she didn't shrink from that challenge, but embraced it. Phiona nodded humbly after each lesson, soaking it all in without much audible response, just as Katwe had trained her to do.

"When we first met, Phiona did not believe in herself," Katende says. "She was nervous and hesitant. She had never had anyone to trust. No one to listen to her. No one to give her time and attention. I realized that her background was affecting her and she was convinced that she could not do anything good. I told her, 'Why do you look down? Look at the person you are talking to in the face. Be yourself. Be free. No one is going to penalize you. No one is going to beat you.' It took several years for her to open up. It wasn't easy."

Ever since the first day Phiona had watched Katende playing with Brian and the other kids in the soccer game at the dump site, she felt as if she could trust him. Katende and Phiona were both kids from the slums who grew up without fathers, struggled for meals, constantly relocated without any tether. He could see himself in her and he tried to make sure she could see herself in him.

"I understood what she was going through because I have gone through that as well," Katende says. "I have always told her what I am. I told her I washed vehicles. She didn't believe it. I told her I walked ten kilometers every day to go to school. She didn't believe it. I used my life experiences to show her a good example."

Katende used their time together at the chessboard to pose some challenging questions to Phiona about her place in the world.

"Are you happy with the life you are leading?" he once asked Phiona.

"No," Phiona said.

"Put yourself in your mom's place, would you like to lead a life like she's leading?"

"No," Phiona said.

"Would you like to make a change?"

"Yes," Phiona said.

"What do you need to do to do that?"

He explained about discipline and good behavior and seizing any opportunity that comes her way and using her past as motivation for her future.

"I told her what has helped me be who I am is that I knew who I was," Katende says. "Because of who I was, if I was not to work hard, I wouldn't be where I am."

They played the game together constantly, Phiona and Katende, often until it was just the two of them left in the project and long past the time when Katende had planned to go home.

While Katende often helped Phiona with advice on which move to play, during one game he deliberately told her to make a poor move. Phiona began to move the piece and then hesitated.

"I told you to do this and you are refusing?" Katende said. "Why?"

"Coach, I think it is a wrong move," Phiona said. "My piece would be captured."

"Have you ever done something wrong because someone else has told you to do it without thinking?" Katende asked her. "Before you do something, always think, 'What will be the repercussions? What will be the consequences?'"

At first, when he played games against Phiona, Katende played as a teacher. He would play her without his queen, or remove his bishops or some pawns from the board, until the time came when he needed all of his pieces to defeat her. Then Phiona started beating him. "Initially I sometimes would give her a chance to capture pieces to see if she can be in position to see a move," Katende says. "Can she capitalize on an advantage like that? I tested her with some tricky moves and she would see them all. I would leave my queen deliberately vulnerable to find out if she could see that it was a trap. Before long, I realized that Phiona could see everything."

Phiona grew more and more comfortable with the game, even teasing her coach, something she would never have felt comfortable doing with any of the boys in the project. She would say things like, "Coach, I see what you are planning and I'm very sorry, but I can't allow you to do that."

Chess began to make sense for Phiona. It is a game of survival through considered aggression. It is about finding some clarity among the confusion, some way to organize the chaos by always thinking several moves ahead of the danger. Phiona has even become a student of the game, writing down each move of her tournament games and reviewing them extensively with Katende afterward. She knows that the best way for her to keep learning is through practice. She is a tireless grinder. When asked to estimate how many games she has played since joining the project, Phiona says she can't imagine a number that high.

"I do believe why she's successful is because she has an open mind to learn," Katende says. "She admires better players and asks herself, 'Can I sometime be like this?' I always tell her it is not enough to want to be like them, you must work like them. Because you don't just wake up one day and you are there."

Katende taught Phiona to understand the game, then to appreciate the game, and then finally to love the game. "One thing I really enjoy about chess is it sharpens my brain," Phiona says. "Before I played chess I wasn't motivated to think, but when I learned the game I really liked how it gave me so many challenges. I feel so comfortable when I am at the board. Even when I lose, I don't want to leave the board. I feel a happiness whenever I am playing the game, doing what I do best."

"There were some dogs in a pack and one of them was much faster than the other dogs. So these dogs would run after cats and eat them. Unfortunately there was a certain cat that was so fast and most of the dogs would run after it and fail to get it. So one time the fastest dog, who liked to show off his speed, was challenged by the other dogs.

"'Hey, there is one cat who is very fast. Do you think you can catch it?'

"'Many times before you have challenged me and I have always caught the cat,' the fastest dog said. 'This cat will be my meal for today.'

"So that day the cat came by. 'Hey, Mr. Cat is there,' said one of the dogs. 'That is the fast one.'

"The fastest dog ran after the cat. He was gone for a long time and finally came back and he hadn't caught the cat. So the other dogs asked, 'What happened?'

"'Me, I was just running for a meal that I can get somewhere else. That cat was running for its life.'"

Katende tells the story with admiration for the unlikely hero, making it clear all along that he is rooting for the cat. "That cat was running to save his life and didn't have any other choice," Katende says. "Phiona looks at chess the same way. I feel maybe that is helping her reach her full potential, because she recognizes chess as a way to survive."

Phiona's game is still very raw. She plays almost entirely on instinct, instead of following the various opening, middlegame, and endgame theory utilized by more refined and experienced players. She succeeds because she possesses that precious chess gene that allows her to envision the board many moves ahead and she focuses on the game as if her life depends on it, which in her case it might.

When Phiona sits at a chessboard she reacts just as she once did when fighting with that abusive boy in the neighborhood or getting teased by the other children during her first day in the chess project. She reacts the way Katwe has taught her to react. She attacks.

"She likes to play what I call 'kill me quick' chess," Godfrey Gali says. "Phiona has a very aggressive plan. She surrounds you until you have nowhere to go and then she will squeeze you like a python until you are dead. That aggression in a girl is quite a treasure."

Still, Phiona's ardor can occasionally get the best of her. "If she has a weakness, it's that she can be too eager to move forward, very eager to kill without ammunition," says Dr. George Zirembuzi, Uganda's former national team coach. "In chess if you try for a coup d'état and fail, you will be hung."

Phiona's game plan features aggression that has been honed over time to be more calculating, molded by her many games against Benjamin and Ivan, who taught her that while attacking, you must never neglect defending.

"In the beginning she was an aggressive player who didn't really know how to attack smartly," Benjamin says. "So we tried to teach her how to stop all the mistakes she was doing. Now she's not so aggressive as she was. She's more strategic. When I play with her I have to be so strict and so steady or she will destroy me."

While Phiona's strategy is to back her opponent into a defensive position as soon as possible, over time she has gradually learned how to handle a game that isn't won through her initial assault. "I think she is always planning her attack, but when she sees some responses that might be dangerous, she addresses them ahead of time," Katende says.

"So by the time she is ready to attack, she has addressed everything. She is aware that if the opponent responds in this kind of way, I will do this. If he does this, I will do this. You won't see any serious concentration on her face. She looks very casual, but you better not take any moves she makes for granted because she is always ready to pounce."

Ivan believes Phiona's greatest strength is her patience. "Our games sometimes last many hours and most girls lose interest after thirty minutes," Ivan says. "Girls have lots of excuses. Phiona never loses interest or makes excuses. She's committed. She never gets tired like the other girls."

"One of the weaknesses we find among most kids we train is that they usually play too fast," Gali says. "Kids don't want to take their time to think through certain moves. But Phiona takes her time. Her opponent may make a move where they offer her some big piece like a queen and if you are the kind of player who plays by impulse without thinking through the moves, you'll lose that way. Phiona looks at all the options and then makes the best move. She makes moves that you don't expect from a kid of her age."

"I think she is developing into what we call a strategic player more than a tactical player," Dr. Zirembuzi says. "Strategic players last longer because they use fundamental principles and they aren't easily surprised, while tactical players have many tricks up their sleeves. She plays textbook chess, which leaves a lot of open road ahead."

Phiona is still so early in her learning curve that Uganda's most renowned chess experts like Dr. Zirembuzi and Joachim Okoth believe her potential is staggering. They talk about how most chess players begin with theory and never fully develop the instincts that Phiona relies upon. They marvel at how much better she can become once she learns to interpret and react to the theory that guides the elite players in the game.

"To love the game as much as Phiona does and already be a champion at her age means her future is much bigger than any girl I've ever known," Dr. Zirembuzi says. "When Phiona loses, she really feels hurt and I like that, because that characteristic will help her keep thirsting to get better."

Phiona captured the national junior championship again in 2008. And again in 2009. Then at Katende's 2009 interproject tournament she defeated Samuel Mayanja, the boys' national junior champion, who wept after losing the game, while the girls in the room shouted, "Phiona is now junior champion for boys *and* girls!"

Phiona didn't celebrate that victory, just as she didn't celebrate her first against Joseph Asaba, another boy she had brought to tears. While she is already implausibly talented at a game she has no business being good at, like most women in Uganda, Phiona is uncomfortable sharing what she is really feeling. She tries to answer any questions about herself with a shrug, but when Phiona is compelled to speak, she is unfailingly humble. She realizes that chess makes her stand out, which in Katwe makes her a potential target, so she is conditioned to say as little as possible.

"I'm very careful on how I live my life," Phiona says. "Chess is just a game. I am very aware that if I'm not behaving well, if I put out a lot of pride, I won't be favored by anyone. Life is not a game. In life I have to stay quiet to ensure I get favor from people."

It is a dilemma for Phiona. She is caught somewhere between trying to be better than everybody else and trying not to be better than everybody else.

"Her personality with the outside world is still quite reserved because she feels inferior due to her background," Katende says. "But in chess I am always reminding her that anyone can lift a piece because it is so light. What separates you is where you choose to put it down. Chess is the one thing in Phiona's life she can control. Chess is her one chance to feel superior."

Harriet experienced the prophecy for the first time in 2008. Phiona had qualified to attend the African Junior Chess Championship in South

Africa and was supposed to leave in a week, when one night Harriet had a dream. In her dream Harriet saw a tiny child who was very dark and dirty sitting in her lap on top of Phiona's passport application papers. That child spoke to Harriet and said, *Your girl is not going.*

In the coming days, despite Katende's tireless efforts to accelerate the bureaucratic process, Phiona's passport was issued too late. Phiona did not go.

Then early in the summer of 2009, Harriet experienced a similar prophecy, though she wasn't sure why this time. She wasn't aware of any pending trips for her daughter and didn't really expect Phiona to ever leave Uganda, but once again Harriet found herself experiencing the same dream about a child sitting on some papers in her lap. This time the child's voice carried a different message.

Your girl is going.

Chapter 8
Heaven

Ivan Mutesasira, Robert Katende, Benjamin Mukumbya, and Phiona Mutesi *(left to right)* on the day they returned to Katwe after representing Uganda at the 2009 International Children's Chess Tournament in Sudan.

S he didn't know if the world was round. Or flat. She knew nothing about the world. The outside world. The world beyond Katwe. The slum can seem endless in every direction and there are few landmarks to break up the endless muddle of shacks. Everything in the slum is "just there." And everything beyond that is unimaginable.

Even though Phiona can see the skyscrapers of downtown Kampala from almost anywhere in Katwe, she had spent the first dozen years of her life assuming that everybody else on earth lived just as she did, scrounging for one meal a day, just hoping to get home safely each day so they could try to survive the next one.

So when Katende informed Phiona that her 2009 national junior tournament victory had qualified her to go to Sudan for Africa's inaugural International Children's Chess Tournament later that summer, she didn't take him seriously. *Sudan? What is Sudan?* All Phiona knew was that Sudan was not "just there."

"When I told Phiona about going to Sudan, she looked at me like she knew this coach is joking," Katende says. "She believed she could not go to another country because she was not anyone in our country. She thought there must be some better people who could go there. She told me, 'How can I go to another country? This is impossible. It will never happen. It is not real.'"

"I remember the day Coach Robert told me that I was going, I thought, 'Who am I to be able to go on a plane?'" Phiona says. "I had never expected that I would go anywhere. For sure, I continued to do my training, as always, but I didn't really believe that I was to go anywhere."

The International Children's Chess Tournament was an event for children aged 16 and under organized by FIDE and the United Nations Security Council as part of a peacemaking effort to popularize chess among the children of East and Central Africa. The tournament, which took place in August of 2009, was underwritten by a local petroleum company that sponsored two boys and one girl from each participating country. From all of Uganda, the three children who qualified all came from Robert Katende's tiny chess project in the Katwe slum. Ivan and Benjamin would be Phiona's teammates at the tournament. Several other players who may have qualified dropped out of consideration, refusing to go with a slum kid.

During the summer of 2009, Phiona watched Ivan and Benjamin training intensely so she figured it must be nearing time for another tournament of some kind. On the night before she was to leave for Sudan, according to Katende's instructions Phiona packed all of the clothes she possessed into her tiny rucksack, expecting to go to a local event. Phiona and Brian were alone in the shack that evening. Harriet and Richard spent the night at the market awaiting the early morning purchase of vegetables to sell.

Brian woke up his sister while it was still dark and Phiona told him it was too early to leave. Brian was so excited he couldn't sleep. The two woke up again shortly after dawn and Brian could sense they were late, measuring time by the call to Muslim prayers cascading across the city. Brian told Phiona not to even go wash up, just to put on her clothes. He picked up Phiona's bag and they began walking, but Phiona was moving at her own pace. Brian kept jogging ahead and would sometimes grab his sister's hand to speed her up. He kept telling Phiona she was late, but she knew she had never gone to any tournament this early, so what was the rush? When they reached the veranda, they were 30 minutes late for the scheduled departure. They hustled onto the minibus, the two siblings quarreling over the fact that Phiona's nonchalance might cause her to miss the plane. Phiona still didn't believe she was flying anywhere.

It was only after Phiona boarded the bus and saw that other children from the chess project had come to escort them, that she thought maybe this trip was different. Then she spotted Ivan's mother, Annet

Nakiwala, who used to babysit Phiona and her siblings when their families were neighbors in Katwe. "You are going to the airport in Entebbe," Nakiwala told Phiona. "You are going to board a plane. You are going to eat good food. You are going to win. We are going to be praying for you."

Many of Ivan's and Benjamin's other relatives refused to go to the airport because it was such an unfamiliar place and they were afraid of what might happen to them there.

Phiona stared out the window as the bus exited the slums and connected to Entebbe Road. She knew about the road. She crossed that dusty and chaotic road every time she walked to the Kibuye market, but she had never before been inside a vehicle on that road. She'd once heard that the road led to the airport. Phiona had never been to the airport before. The only time Phiona had ever seen an airplane was in the sky.

The group arrived at the airport in Entebbe and met Godfrey Gali, who would be chaperoning the three children on the trip. Gali watched Phiona as she wandered around the airport awestruck.

"It felt like taking someone from the nineteenth century and plunging them into the present world," Gali says. "Everything at the airport was so strange to her; security cameras, luggage conveyors, so many white people."

Phiona passed through security and looked back through a window at the people who had escorted them to the airport. She waved to Brian and to her first chess tutor, eight-year-old Gloria Nansubuga. When Phiona saw both Brian and Gloria crying she realized that maybe she really was going to this place called Sudan.

"No one else in Katwe could believe they were going," Katende says. "The only way to make it real was to bring some people to the airport with the kids and even when those witnesses came back, they said it might not be true. I even requested to the driver not to leave the airport until they all see the kids' plane leave the ground."

As the plane took off, the three children felt scared and dizzy and Phiona nearly vomited. Then when the plane ascended above the clouds, Phiona looked out the window and asked, "Mr. Gali, are we about to reach Heaven?"

"No," Gali said. "Heaven is a bit higher."

When the flight attendants came by with sandwiches, none of the children had ever seen a sandwich before. They waited for Gali to eat as if he were a food taster and then they still chose not to eat.

"In the airplane I was smiling all the time because I could not believe that I was the one flying to another country," Phiona says. "I felt like I was going to a new world."

By the end of the 90-minute flight to Juba, Sudan, the three children were no longer apprehensive about the travel. They had completely embraced the adventure. Phiona's room at the hotel was like no place she'd ever seen in her life. She stared at the bed. She had never seen one like it. She could not believe she was the one who was going to sleep in that bed. The only one. She had never slept alone in a bed before. She had never seen a television screen attached to a wall and she thought the remote control was magical. It was the first time she'd experienced air-conditioning. The first time she'd ever seen a flushing toilet. She flushed it over and over, fascinated by how the water spun and disappeared. "I could never have imagined this place I was visiting," Phiona says. "I felt like a queen."

Benjamin and Ivan were placed next door to Phiona, who was rooming with a girl from Kenya. Phiona could not speak to her roommate because Phiona's English was not sufficient to carry on a conversation. The unfamiliar surroundings again filled all of the Ugandan kids with anxiety. "Whenever one of us got a bit nervous we would keep encouraging each other," Ivan says. "One of us would say, 'This is where we're going to stay. This is so good. This is where we're going to sleep.' Everyone was comforting each other."

When they went for lunch in the hotel restaurant, they were each handed menus and Gali told them they could ask for whatever they wanted. Phiona didn't understand that she was being given a choice about what to eat for the first time. The children pointed to everything they could recognize. Chicken. Fish. Pork. They wanted to order it all. Gali told them they should ask for only what they would be able to finish. When it came time for Phiona to order, she said, "Let me have a big fish."

The fish stretched across her plate and Phiona could not come close to finishing it, but Ivan told her she must. She gave the remainder to him, but Ivan could not eat it all. The portions were simply too large for children accustomed to rationed meals.

As the lunch ended, Phiona said, "Mr. Gali, I'm going to do my best playing chess so that I may come back to such a place."

The day before the three kids left Kampala for Sudan, Benjamin approached Robert Katende at the chess project with a worried look on his face. "Coach, I'm scared," Benjamin said. "What makes us think we can win any games when none of us has ever even reached the airport? What's going to happen if we lose?"

Katende gathered Benjamin, Ivan and Phiona around him and shared the story of Shadrach, Meshach, and Abednego from scripture:

> "These three guys refused to worship idols, so King Nebuchadnezzar passed a decree that said that all the people must submit to the king and to worship what he said should be worshipped. But these guys believed in God and they didn't want to worship any idols. These guys would not submit, so the king said if you're not willing to worship idols, I will set you in a furnace. So he commanded that they set afire a furnace and the guys said we must continue to believe in our God and we know he has the ability to save us, but even if he does not, we are not ready to submit to the idols. So the king was bitter and he commanded his people to set a furnace seven times hotter than it had ever been set and the three guys were sent into the furnace. The three guys didn't burn up and when

the king looked in the furnace there was a fourth person inside. A divine person. It could have been God or an angel. It was a fearful moment, but these three put their trust in God no matter what comes and God was able to rescue them from the fire. If you have great fear the question is, 'Where do you put your trust?' You trust in God. Even if you lose, you honor yourself by competing and we're going to honor you."

Though he didn't share his expectations with the children, Katende wasn't at all concerned with their results in the tournament.

"The moment those three kids from Katwe were able to fly on a plane to another country, that was already the ultimate win I was looking for," Katende says. "I did not expect them to perform well in Sudan. I was just looking for them to be exposed to that kind of atmosphere."

"I know I didn't expect them to do much," Gali says. "I knew they would try their best. I knew they wouldn't be outclassed completely. Some of the other teams had better training and more experience in international events. Our team had none. I was trying to encourage them that even if you lose, don't give up. I was preparing them for the worst-case scenario."

In the tournament, the Ugandan trio, by far the youngest team in the competition, played against teams from 16 other African nations. When the pairings were announced, Phiona learned that she was going to play Isabelle Asiema from Kenya in the opening game. She'd heard the tournament administrators praise Asiema, believing that she was one of the most talented young female players in all of Africa and clearly the best girl in the tournament. At the time Phiona didn't realize that Asiema was also her roommate. "I was really very nervous," Phiona says, "I heard people talking about a Kenyan girl who was playing very well and I felt like it caused me to have a lot of fear and I felt discouraged to even go and play her."

The three Ugandans hatched a plan to engage the Kenyan team

in friendly games on the day before the tournament officially began as a means of scouting them. Phiona played Kenya's top-ranked boy, Benjamin played their second-ranked boy, and Ivan played Asiema. "I beat their best boy and then I wondered if this guy was just trying to trick me," Phiona says. "Maybe he just wanted to see how I play and he was just fooling around. So I played a second game with him and I won again."

After the friendly games against the Kenyans, the three Ugandans huddled to discuss what they'd learned. Phiona anxiously asked Ivan, "How was their girl?"

Ivan said that he'd beaten her in every game they'd played. Then Ivan told Phiona, "You are going to beat that girl."

"But Ivan," Phiona said, "just because you've beaten her doesn't mean I will beat her."

"No, you are going to beat that girl," Ivan said. "I know how you play and now I have played that girl and I know you can beat her."

Phiona and Benjamin then reported that they had won their friendly games as well. "All of a sudden I realized that if they are not tricking us we will be in position to challenge these people," Benjamin recalls. "So in a way we tried to comfort each other that way."

The next morning, when the time came for the tournament to begin, Phiona's nerves had returned. Her hands shook whenever she lifted a piece. Her body shivered. Her legs quaked beneath the table. Asiema executed a well-trained opening. Phiona, who had little training in formal openings, simply pushed her pieces forward with her basic plan of how to defend them. When they reached the middlegame, Phiona had systematically built a position advantage and realized that she was actually squeezing her opponent. Feeling the pressure, Asiema then started making errors. "I could actually wonder, 'Is this move she made like a trick or is it actually a mistake?'" Phiona says. "I realized that they were blunders and I continued to pin her down and capture her pieces that were unprotected."

After a very long game, Phiona reduced Asiema to just her king on the board. Then Phiona cornered that king with a rook and several pawns until Asiema was finally checkmated.

"I got courage from beating that girl and how everyone was praising me," Phiona says. "That gave me the belief that I could beat the rest."

In the next game, Phiona played against the top-seeded Kenyan male player, and she beat him just as she had in the practice games. "That boy wanted to cry when she finished him," Gali said. "You could see the expression on his face and it looked like he couldn't believe it."

"The games got harder because the other coaches would tell their players about our tactics and give their players tactics to try to win or make draws," Benjamin says. "But we kept telling each other, 'We can make it. We can make it.'"

Benjamin recalls one game when he was in a very disadvantaged position against a strong player. Gali was speaking with somebody else watching the game and Benjamin overheard Gali say, "It seems that Uganda is going to lose this point."

"I made a move which I had not seen before that blocked his bishop and then he had no way of stopping my pawn from passing and I somehow won that game," Benjamin says. "For sure, I don't know how I made that great move, but I think it must be through the power of the Holy Spirit. I felt like it was not me making the moves."

"After three matches or so everyone in the tournament started talking about who was strong, so when they met them they knew they were facing a superior opponent and they became a bit timid," Gali says. "That's when I first thought we could be winning this. Everybody there was scared of ours. Ours were a class above."

None of the Ugandan players actually thought about winning the tournament. It never occurred to them. They just kept playing. Phiona played eight games without a loss. Benjamin and Ivan were undefeated as well.

After their final games, they returned to their rooms and soon after, Gali entered Ivan and Benjamin's room to tell them that Uganda had been declared the tournament champions. From her room next door,

Phiona could hear Ivan and Benjamin shouting. She joined the others and the three started screaming and jumping up and down on the beds.

At the closing ceremonies the Ugandans received gold medals, certificates, and a trophy. "Winning felt amazing," Ivan says. "We couldn't even believe it. It was such a surprise at first, but then we somehow reflected as if it was a normal thing because in Uganda we'd all experienced winning. I remember Phiona was thinking about her mother and brother and how good they would feel."

A stunned Russian chess administrator approached Phiona after the tournament and told her, "I have a son who is an International Master and he was not as good at your age as you are."

Meanwhile several of the opposing coaches approached Gali and asked, "How do you train these kids?"

"I thought to myself," Gali recalls with a chuckle, "'if only they knew where these kids are coming from.'"

When the ceremony ended, Ivan asked Gali, "Now that we've won this one, where do we go next? Are we going to another country?" The children hoped there was another tournament, a new place to visit, but Gali told them it was time to go home. Ivan collected soap, shampoo, and a pen from his hotel room as gifts for his mother.

Through it all, Katende had received regular updates from Gali through text messages. Katende marveled at the progress of his players. One day he received a text that read, *Robert, I am surprised to tell you that these kids have got gold medals. They are the champions for this tournament.*

"When I learned that they had won I went and told some people at the Sports Outreach office and they didn't believe it," Katende says. "They thought it was a fake. They were suspicious. It was really very unbelievable. In Katwe some people said this is a lie. It cannot happen. They know these kids' situations and they ask, 'So how? How?'"

Katende concentrated on what the unlikely victory would mean moving forward. "To me I was so excited because I knew this was going to be a big landmark to restore hope and to inspire the minds of everyone in the chess project," Katende says. "Most people in the slums think they can't do something, but if success happens, then people have a reference to build on. I knew this would be a foundation for each and every thing that we will do in the future."

When the Ugandan delegation returned to Kampala the following afternoon, Katende met them at the airport. The three children were smiling and carrying a trophy that was too big to fit into any of their tiny backpacks. When Katende initially tried to congratulate Phiona, she was too busy laughing and teasing her teammates, something he had never seen her do before. For once, he realized, Phiona was just being the kid that she is.

If only that story could end there. Two slum kids, coach and pupil, each at some time left for dead, combining to win a most improbable championship. But happy endings are as rare as snow in Katwe.

"I remember when we arrived back at the airport in Uganda and the plane inside it is always conditioned to stay cool, but the moment I left the airport I felt the sun scorching me," Benjamin says. "I said to Ivan, 'Can we go back?'"

"I felt bad, too," Ivan says. "I just thought of where we were heading and I knew that things were about to be turned upside down because we are leaving this place that was so fantastic and we are coming back to Katwe. But I had no choice. I just had to endure it because this is our home."

"It felt like I was going back to a kind of prison," Phiona says.

As Phiona, Benjamin, and Ivan were driven back into Katwe for a victory celebration, the psychological shift began to take hold. They became apprehensive about what they were going to find when they arrived there. Windows in their van were reflexively shut and backpacks pushed out of sight. Ivan, who was holding the trophy in his lap, suddenly slid it under the seat in front of him. The faces that had been so joyful at the airport turned solemn, the mask of the slum. The three children discussed who would keep the trophy and decided none of them could because it would surely be stolen, so they asked Katende if he could lock it in the storage shed.

Arriving at the site of the chess project, they were surprised to find children waiting there singing and dancing and chanting: *Uganda! Uganda! Uganda!* The three champions looked embarrassed, totally unaccustomed to being treated as heroes. Brian lifted Phiona onto his shoulders and joyously carried her around in the street until she begged him to put her down. Rodney Suddith took a few photographs that reveal all of the children smiling and laughing except for Ivan, Benjamin, and Phiona, who each look as if they would rather be anywhere else. "It was as if they'd done something that they really thought was going to change their lives, but then it really doesn't," Suddith says. "The sense I got was their disappointment that they were right back where they started. They had had their moment. But that moment was gone."

The excitement in the crowd that afternoon existed not only because the three children from the slum had won an international chess tournament, but because some people from Katwe had gone away and come back. The children were greeted with some strange questions:

Did you fly on the silver bird?
Did you stay indoors or in the bush?
Why did you come back here?

"It struck me how difficult it must have been for them to go to another world and return," Suddith says. "Sudan might as well be the moon to people in the slum who have no point of reference. The three kids couldn't share their experience with the others because they just couldn't connect. It puzzled me at first and then it made me sad, and then I wondered, 'Is what they have done really a good thing?'"

As Phiona left the celebration headed for her home that evening, a mzungu excitedly asked her, "What is the first thing you're going to say to your mother?"

"I need to ask her," Phiona said, "'Do we have enough food for breakfast?'"

Chapter 9
The Other Side

Phiona Mutesi relishes her first victory at the 2010 Chess Olympiad
in Khanty-Mansiysk, Russia.

P hiona did not eat the night she returned from Sudan. Or the day after. Neither did Benjamin or Ivan. For once, it wasn't because they couldn't. It was because they didn't want to. A big fish was no longer an option. In fact, there were no options. They had sampled from the tree of knowledge and their appetites had changed forever. They didn't know it yet, but none of their lives would ever be quite the same.

There is a stubborn tolerance amid the misery of a place like Katwe. A subconscious defiance that is necessary to keep going. It is a peculiar disconnect between circumstance and attitude that creates a uniquely African peace of mind. Many have argued that the average African is more serene than the average American, and much of the reason has to do with access. Many people in Katwe do not know there is anything better for which to strive, which leads to an odd kind of tranquility, which some might call lethargy. Every day people like Phiona Mutesi walk a fine line between quiet forbearance and hopelessness, a line that had to be redrawn when Phiona saw what she saw in Sudan.

From her relatively plush hotel room in Juba, Phiona returned home to a 10 x 10 foot windowless room, its walls made of crumbling brick with a corrugated tin roof held up by some spindly wood beams and spiderwebs. Drawn across the doorway was a curtain, which must almost always remain open in the oppressive heat of a country dissected by the equator. Laundry hung on wash lines that crisscrossed the room. There was nothing on the walls, except where someone had etched some phone numbers in case of emergency. There was no phone.

The entire contents of the home were two jugs for water, a wash bin, a kerosene lamp, a tiny charcoal stove made from scrap metal, a teapot, a few plates and cups, one well-worn toothbrush, a tiny shard of a mirror, a Bible, and two musty mattresses stacked on top of each other, which were spread out at night to accommodate the four people who regularly slept in the shack: Phiona, Harriet, Brian, and Richard.

A piece of warped plywood covered the only small window. There were a few intended air holes in the brick for ventilation and a few unintended holes in the roof that didn't provide much shelter from the torrential rains that often struck at night. Outside was a broom that Harriet used to sweep the pebbles off the mud stoop. Just beyond the stoop was a pit that served as a garbage dump where roosters pecked away at the debris of rotten banana peels and dung. Around the corner were three pieces of tin bent together to form a rudimentary bathing area just a few paces from a brick outhouse that drained into a hole in the ground and down the hill into the valley.

Four small pouches of rice, curry powder, salt, and tea leaves were the only hints of food in the house. There was no electricity because Harriet couldn't afford the 20,000 shillings a month it took to pirate it.

Back in the shack on the night she returned from Sudan, Phiona felt a fever as she watched Brian and Richard eat small bowls of rice. Brian asked Phiona, "What kind of food do people in Sudan eat?" Phiona changed the subject. Then Brian asked, "How does it feel to be in a plane?" Again, Phiona's answer was brief. Finally, Brian asked, "How do you pee in a plane?" Phiona couldn't resist smiling at the question and tried a bit harder this time to satisfy her brother's curiosity, but her heart was still not in it. Living in her shack felt different somehow. She was a changed person. "When Phiona came back there was a lot of work to be done at home, but we treated her like a big, important person in the family," Brian says. "I realized it was really very hard for Phiona to participate in any kind of work because she spent most of the time in Sudan not doing anything. She didn't want to do chores, so I and Richard had to endure about two weeks when we were doing all of her work for her."

Phiona didn't see Harriet her first night back from Sudan. Her mother was off at the market. Harriet didn't arrive home until very late that night and left again early the following morning before Phiona woke up. Phiona wouldn't see her mother for two days. When the family finally reunited, Harriet didn't know what had transpired in Sudan. "Mama," Brian said, "are you aware that when Phiona left that she had won?"

"What?" Harriet said, raising her arms to the heavens. "She won? Let me go to the church and testify. God is so good!"

Harriet immediately left for church. When she returned an hour later, she was still brimming with pride. "You see?" she told Brian. "You wanted to stop your sister from going to the chess program. You see? You see now what she can do?"

It wasn't easy to return to school either. The morning after coming home from Sudan, Phiona grabbed the green plastic bag she used as her school backpack and walked five kilometers through Katwe to the Universal Junior Primary School, where she was a student in P7. Universal was a cramped, dusty place where the latrines dominated the schoolyard, their foul smell permeating the compound. The school bell was the rusty rim of a tire, with a crowbar attached on a string. At the beginning of each school day the children sang "We Shall Overcome."

On the morning Phiona returned, the school staged a brief ceremony to congratulate her. Phiona still had a little money left over from a small allowance she'd been given for the tournament in Sudan, so she quietly distributed some coins among the poorest classmates at her school. "When I saw that, I admired her heart," says Zakaba Al-Abdal, the school's headmaster. "I thought that this girl will make a very good future woman." After witnessing the positive effect of chess on Phiona, the headmaster added chess to Universal's curriculum, the classes taught by Benjamin three times a week.

Winning the tournament in Sudan prompted Phiona to become even more obsessed with chess. The next scheduled event was a national tournament beginning in November that would include all of the top players in Uganda. Phiona begged Katende to let her play, but he refused, knowing it was a qualifying tournament for the Chess Olympiad. Katende believed Phiona and his other chess apprentices weren't ready to handle that level of competition against much older and more experienced players. "I feared," Katende says. "I was sure Phiona could not qualify because I knew who those other girls are and I thought they were definitely stronger than she is. I thought it was a waste of time and finances."

But a week before the tournament began, Katende received a phone call from Godfrey Gali asking him to enter Phiona in the tournament field. Gali didn't view Phiona as a serious contender to qualify, but he wanted her to help strengthen the players who would qualify.

Says Katende, "I told Phiona, 'Mr. Gali is insisting that I enter you, but I'm doing so on grounds that you are going for training. Those big ladies who are playing, they will be competing to see who represents the country, but you just go and that will be good training as they are preparing for that tournament.'"

Gali had sold Katende on the idea that it would benefit Phiona to be introduced to the tournament before she attempted to qualify for a future Olympiad. Katende was thinking two years ahead, to 2012. Then Phiona would be more comfortable in the pressurized atmosphere of an event like that. He believed her level at least approached that of her competition, so Phiona was the only player from Katende's chess project he would enter into the event, while other players like Ivan and Benjamin were held out.

"Coach knew I would have to play against those big ladies," Phiona says. "At first he was very sure that he would not allow me to go and play, but I really wanted to go there and try to improve my game, so he allowed it."

The qualifying tournament took place over a period of three months, one game each Saturday. The women's field included ten players who played a round-robin and the top five overall finishers would qualify for the Olympiad. Katende did not attend the early rounds. He sent Phiona with his assistant, Paul Mubiru, because Katende was busy tending to the other children in the chess project on Saturdays. On the first Saturday of qualifying, Phiona came back to the veranda and said, "Coach, I won."

"You won?" Katende said. "That is good."

Katende knew there were six women in the field who were clearly the best players and assumed that Phiona had played against a weaker opponent. The next Saturday Phiona returned to the project and reported that she'd won again. "I still wasn't taking it seriously," Katende says. "I took a look at the game she played on her recording sheet and I told her, 'This was a good game. You played well.' But I still knew she could not qualify."

Through five of the nine games of the qualifying tournament, Phiona produced three wins, one draw and one loss. At that point, Gali phoned Katende. "Robert, we are all surprised," Gali said, "but it seems this little girl might even qualify when we see the trend of this tournament."

"How?" Katende asked.

"She has played most of the strong people and she has actually challenged them," Gali said. "If she continues to play this way, there's no way she can miss to be among the five people who are needed."

"Are you sure?" Katende said. "Are you serious about that?"

He asked if Phiona had been told. Gali said she had not.

Katende later told Phiona, "You know that you might qualify to go to Russia? Now, it's a must. Let us intensify our training and make sure that you win all of the remaining games. If you win those games, you will qualify."

Katende reviewed all of the games Phiona had previously played in the tournament. He asked the strongest boys in the Katwe project, Benjamin, Ivan, and Richard, to play a game against Phiona every day. Katende also tried to play at least one game against her each day.

Katende received email updates on the standings each week. With three games remaining he calculated that even if Phiona lost all of her remaining games, she would still qualify. Phiona became the first to clinch qualification for the Olympiad and during her final games, she even had some of the older women begging her to draw with them so that they could qualify as well. Phiona finished in second place overall. Unaware that the tournament winner would also be considered Uganda's national champion, Phiona gave away a game at the end of the event that she thought had no meaning, but instead cost her the national title.

"The qualifying for the Olympiad was very tight because everybody who participated was very good, very strong, and everyone wanted to go so badly," says Rita Nsubuga, who also qualified. "I admit I feared Phiona. I would rather play someone I know than a young kid, because you get disappointed when a young kid beats you. All of the other girls were fearing her. They knew that this one is a threat."

"It was exciting, but with Uganda many things had happened before when qualifying for a tournament came to nothing," Katende says. "Because it is Uganda, I didn't really believe that Phiona was going to Russia. Uganda had never before been able to afford to send a women's team to the Chess Olympiad. I told her, 'If God makes it possible for you, you might go.' I never said she *will* go. I didn't think she would."

Several months passed before Gali informed Katende that FIDE would pay for all ten of Uganda's players to travel to Russia. When Katende shared that news with Sports Outreach, Rodney Suddith began raising funds to send Katende, because Phiona was too young to travel to Russia without him. When those funds materialized, as one of the few Ugandan delegates who could afford the trip, Katende was nominated to be the women's team captain.

In early September, Universal Junior Primary School received a letter from the Uganda Chess Federation requesting Phiona's release from school for a month so that she could play in the Chess Olympiad. The school's headmaster made a dozen copies of the letter and posted them in each classroom as a means of inspiration.

On her final day at school before leaving for Russia, the school declared its own holiday. In Phiona's class 33 students were packed into a sweltering classroom. On the wall were posters of Africa and of the presidents of Uganda, and a map of the world. When the students were asked to point out where Phiona was going on the map, only one was able to correctly identify Russia. Phiona was among the rest who could not.

On the day before the Ugandan national team was due to leave for the Olympiad, the Uganda Chess Federation staged a send-off press conference. There were no microphones, so the reporters and players in the audience had to lean forward in their plastic chairs to try to hear the speeches from the dignitaries.

"You are ten Ugandans," said Jasper Aligawesa, the general secretary of Uganda's National Council of Sports, "but you leave behind thirty million Ugandans whose eyes are on you."

Federation chairman Joseph Kaamu told the players how in 1972 he remembered Idi Amin sending the Ugandan national boxing team off to an international competition by saying, "Don't try to win on points. Just knock the guy out and you will have no doubt who wins." Then Kaamu seemed to undercut his pep talk by saying, "When you get to the Olympiad, we know you will never beat the Russians, but try your best."

The following day a half dozen children from the chess project, many of whom had never ridden in a vehicle before, accompanied Phiona to the airport. When Night's three-year-old daughter Rita saw Phiona leave with white people, the alarmed child mimicked a common warning in Uganda about running off with strangers: "The mzungus have taken Phiona and they are going to cut off her head!"

On the bus to the airport Phiona teased Katende about how this would be his first time on an airplane, so Phiona would act as the coach for this journey.

Phiona's mother also accompanied her to the airport, her first ever trip there. Harriet had some final advice for her daughter. "Be careful," she told Phiona. "The country you are going to is not your own. If you behave well you will represent your country well. If not, you will have let your country down. Don't be misled by anyone, especially boys, and a lot of treasures lie ahead of you. God is remembering us."

Then after wiping away her tears with a rag, Harriet rubbed Phiona's shoulders and said something she had never said to her before: "Stay warm."

Harriet would later admit that she didn't believe she would ever see her daughter again.

They flew through one night and into the next, through Nairobi, Kenya, and Dubai in the United Arab Emirates, and didn't breathe fresh air again until the chill wind of Khanty-Mansiysk, Russia. Phiona had traveled from the only world she'd ever known to the middle of nowhere. From a place where she'd spent nearly every day of her life to a place she could never have imagined spending a single day of her life. Siberia.

As she stared out the airplane window during the final hours of the flight, she saw nothing in every direction. She couldn't believe there was so much open space with no people living there, nothing built on it. Khanty-Mansiysk is an oil town of about 75,000 stolid citizens on the stark Siberian steppe, so isolated, so far from any other metropolitan area that it has no bus station or railway.

The first thing Phiona noticed about Siberia was that her initial fear back when she'd first learned about the trip had been confirmed. It was cold there. Very cold. She was warned that on the warmest day she'd spend in Khanty-Mansiysk, the temperature wouldn't reach the coldest temperatures she'd ever experienced in Uganda. She also noticed that the streets were well paved, devoid of the dust that she had grown so accustomed to at home. There were traffic lights but no traffic. The people were all so smartly dressed. There were so many tall buildings. Even the bus she rode from the airport to the hotel was nothing like any vehicle she'd ever seen before. The hotel was so big it was hard to remember how to find her room. She took a shower and at first the water came out freezing cold and she wondered why anyone would ever want to do that, until it was pointed out to her that there was a faucet for hot water as well. In the lobby there were people of many races, all speaking languages she could not understand.

Katende sensed this was a much bigger culture shock for Phiona than her trip to Sudan and as he watched his pupil wander around wide-eyed he kept reminding her that while everything else may be different, when the tournament began the chessboard would still be familiar—the same 64 squares she tried to conquer every day in Katwe.

The Chess Olympiad is the world's premier international team chess championship. It began in 1927 and has been staged 39 times in all, including biennially since 1950. It comprises the best chess players in the world. Former world champions Anatoly Karpov, Garry Kasparov, and Bobby Fischer all competed in at least four Olympiads. Before 2010, the previous 15 Olympiads were all won by Russia or countries once part of the Soviet Union. Russia's leadership in the sport helped Khanty-Mansiysk develop into a chess hub in recent years, hosting the 2005, 2007, and 2009 Chess World Cups and earning the right to host the Olympiad through a bidding system similar to that of the Olympic Games.

Uganda has participated in every Chess Olympiad since 1980 except the 1990 Moscow Olympiad, but never had a Ugandan woman played in the tournament. The Uganda Chess Federation often struggled to finance a full men's team. A women's team had never seriously been considered until FIDE announced they would pay for both a men's and a women's team to travel to the 2010 event.

The Olympiad format consists of national teams competing against each other in one match per day. Four players compete for each team, beginning with the top players on Board 1 through the fourth-rated players on Board 4. Each player is awarded one point for a game won and a half point for a game drawn. Cumulative points in all four games determine which country wins the match. One player on each team sits out each day. For most of the Olympiad, Phiona would play Board 2 because that is where she ranked among the five women who qualified for the Ugandan team.

Uganda's big ladies knew nothing about the little girl. Phiona's Olympiad teammates were all from a different world. All of them grew up in more affluent neighborhoods of Kampala. All of them graduated from college, including three from Makerere University, one of the finest schools in all of East Africa. They were all groomed to have careers. None of them had ever been to Katwe.

Rita Nsubuga, 25, learned the game as a child from her father who had played against some of Uganda's elite players such as Dr. George Zirembuzi and Joachim Okoth. She won her first chess tournament in primary school, earning a small magnetic chessboard as a prize, and she became enamored with the game. Rita's father would place a 20,000-shilling note beside the family chessboard and tell his daughter that if she could beat him, the money was hers. Once when Rita won a tournament, her father rewarded her by taking her on a cruise. Eventually Rita began training under Zirembuzi and became the first girl ever to join his chess club, the Mulago Kings, which helped her to qualify for the 2008 Olympiad in Germany, but the funds were not there to send a women's team.

Joan Butindo, 27, started playing chess after spending many evenings watching her mother and father play games that sometimes spread out over three or four days. Joan often found herself driven by the urge to change one or two pieces from the positions where they were left overnight, which alerted Joan's father to her interest in the game. He gave her lessons and they played regularly. By the age of 11, Joan had become the best player in her family, telling all of her siblings that she was no longer interested in playing the "dirty games," only chess. By the age of 23, Joan had become Uganda's national women's champion.

Ivy Claire Amoko, 24, learned chess from her stepbrother when she was 11 years old, but she initially found it dull. Ivy didn't play again until age 14 during a competition at boarding school, where she lost her first game and promptly quit. She wouldn't return to chess until

2007, when the 19-year-old was invited to participate in an inter-hall competition at university. Ivy shocked herself by winning her first game and has continued in the sport ever since, viewing chess as a welcome diversion from her work as a law student. She distinctly recalls playing in a tournament, losing to Joan Butindo—then the national champion—and hearing later that Joan had said she was a weak player. Ivy dedicated herself to training, eventually beat Joan, and became the women's national champion in 2010, finishing ahead of Phiona at the Olympiad qualifying event.

Grace Kigeni, 24, learned the game from a friend during a school holiday when she was 13. She played in some tournaments during secondary school, but didn't dedicate herself to the game until joining Rita playing for a club at Makerere University and then the Mulago Kings.

When the big ladies were asked about Phiona before the Olympiad began, they all agreed that she possessed amazing potential, but there were times when Phiona didn't seem invested enough in the game, when she reacted to a loss with a dismissive shrug of the shoulders.

"I don't know her background or how she started in chess," Grace says. "I don't know if she wanted to play or if she was made to play. That is what is different with us. If I didn't want to play, I wouldn't play. Nobody is going to force me to play. I really see a difference for her. Maybe she feels like chess must save her. When I'm around her, she's just like any other child. A little carefree. I sense her passion is really sunk in. She knows how important chess can be for her, but she doesn't like to show it."

"The attitude Phiona gives us is that she doesn't care that much," Ivy says. "It's like she has a wall that she is always trying to hide behind so no one knows what she's thinking or what she's feeling. She's a tough person and she probably thinks breaking down will make her look weak, so she's blocking away so much emotion that would probably help her. I just wish she would show she cares."

Phiona admits that she doesn't reveal herself to her teammates very often. It is a product of Katwe and they wouldn't understand.

"Actually it is very true that no one can see me inside," Phiona says. "Sometimes when I lose I can even smile and put on a happy face, but inside I'm in real pain because I never want to lose any game. If you look at me, it is very hard to know that I am going through some challenges unless I have told you. It is part of living in the slums. At home we may not have much, but we remain proud, because we fear being abused for showing how we feel. That's how our mother brought us up. During bad times we just keep it to ourselves and we don't show it out. We swallow that pain."

Phiona cried. Sobbed uncontrollably. After her second game at the 2010 Chess Olympiad, a game against a Taiwanese player that she knew she should have won, Phiona Mutesi was inconsolable.

Phiona could not remember the last time she cried, but she couldn't control herself. She somehow felt it was safe to cry in Siberia, so far away from home, so she buried her head in her pillow and bawled. Let it all out. Her teammates, Rita and Grace and Ivy and Joan, they all tried to comfort her. Katende tried to reassure her. But Phiona's tears just kept flowing all through the night, as if because she was in a place where she was permitted to cry, she was going to make up for all of the sadness she had never been allowed to indulge in Katwe.

"When Phiona reached the Olympiad she may have thought the things she was doing to win games in Uganda would be the same things she'd do to win games there," Rita says. "But that was not the case. So maybe she got a bit disappointed. She made a mistake to lose that second game, but we tried not to say things that insult her. We tried to encourage her."

"When she lost that game it was kind of a shock to us because we knew she was good enough to win it," Grace says. "The environment was tough on her. She was so young. The board she was playing on was quite high. We were all talking about, 'How could you put such a young girl on such a board?' We were all scared and intimidated because we had not been exposed to that level of competition. Like all of us, I'm sure Phiona looked back at that game and some of the poor moves she made and thought, 'Oh my God, what was I thinking?'"

Katende decided that to relieve some stress on Phiona, he would sit her out of the next day's match against Japan. Phiona looked on as her team registered its first match victory by winning one game and drawing the other three. Katende believed that had he let Phiona play she would likely have won her game, which left him even more conflicted about whether to play Phiona in the next match against Brazil, a stronger opponent. Katende rested Phiona again, believing that she hadn't completely stabilized and hoping to bring her back against weaker competition.

Chess. Chess. Chess. Even when Phiona did not play, she did not escape. After a long day of chess at the Olympiad, the players would return to the hotel and talk about chess. If they were not talking chess, they were playing it and if a laptop computer was open, chances are that a chessboard was on the screen. Even when she was not playing, Phiona was engulfed by chess, interrupted only by visits to the hotel restaurant, where she dined on three meals a day at an all-you-can-eat buffet. At the first few meals, Phiona made herself sick by overeating. Even during dinners, chess moves were replayed with salt and pepper shakers.

Chess is not a spectator sport. Other than teammates and coaches, only a few family members and an occasional reporter watch the Olympiad matches play out. During games, it is not uncommon for 20 minutes to elapse without a single move. Players regularly leave the game for a bathroom break or to get a cup of tea or perhaps to psyche out an opponent by pretending it isn't even necessary to sit at the board to win. Phiona never left the board. She didn't know what it meant to psyche out an opponent or, fortunately for her, what it meant to be psyched out.

She was restless. Games at the Olympiad progressed too slowly for Phiona, nothing like chess back in Katwe. She had spent two games fidgeting and slouching in her seat, desperate for her opponents to get on with it.

Wary of Phiona's breakdown after the second game, Katende quietly rued the Uganda Chess Federation's decision to place Phiona as her team's Board 2 player. That meant Phiona must face elite players from other teams rather than lower-seeded competition with less experience whom he suspected she could be defeating.

Phiona's third game was against a Woman Grandmaster from Egypt, Mona Khaled. Pleased by Khaled's quick pace of play, Phiona got lured into her opponent's rhythm and played too fast, causing her to make critical errors. Khaled played flawlessly, winning the game in just 24 moves. When Phiona conceded after less than an hour, Katende looked worried, but Phiona recognized that on this day she was beaten by an exceptional player. Instead of being discouraged, she was inspired. Phiona walked straight over to Katende and said, "Coach, I will be a Grandmaster someday."

Phiona looked relieved, and a bit astonished, to have spoken those words.

Phiona's opponent in her fourth game was Sonia Rosalina, an Angolan, who kept staring at Phiona's eyes, which Rosalina would later say were the most competitive she has ever faced in chess. Phiona was behind for most of the game, but she refused to surrender. She battled back and had a chance to force a draw in the endgame, but at the pivotal moment, she played too passively, too defensively, not like herself. After more than three hours and 72 moves, Phiona finally grudgingly submitted, confessing that she didn't have her "courage" when she needed it most. She promised herself that she would never, ever, let that happen again.

The ninth day of the tournament, September 30, 2010, dawned cold and dreary, like every other day at the Olympiad. Phiona hated the

Russian weather, but she loved the hotel room, the clean water, and the three meals a day, and she was already dreading her return home when she would begin scrounging for food again.

Phiona sat down at the chessboard for her fifth game wearing a white knit hat, a black overcoat, and woolly beige boots that were several sizes too large, all gifts from mzungu. Her opponent was an Ethiopian, Haregeweyn Abera, who, like Phiona, was an African teenager and an Olympiad rookie. For the first time in the tournament, Phiona saw someone across the table she could relate to. She saw herself. For the first time in the tournament, she was not intimidated at all.

Phiona played black, the defender in a chess game, but remained patient and gradually shifted the momentum during the first 20 moves until she created an opening to attack. Suddenly Phiona felt as if she were back on the veranda in Katwe, pushing and pushing and pushing Abera's pieces into retreat until there was nowhere left for Abera to move.

When Abera extended her hand in defeat, Phiona tried and failed to suppress her gap-toothed grin. Then Phiona skipped out of the hall, cocked her head back, and unleashed a blissful shriek into the frigid Siberian sky loud enough to startle some of the players still inside the arena. It was a shriek like Phiona had never shrieked before. The shriek of a 14-year-old who could not afford to buy her own chessboard vanquishing one of the better players on the planet and having no experience suppressing that kind of joy. The shriek of a dismissed girl from a dismissed world finally making herself be heard.

"She's only fourteen?" Rashida Corbin asked incredulously. "This is her first Olympiad? For a fourteen-year-old kid with no formal coaching to be playing that confidently on Board 2 at the Olympiad, that's fantastic. I commend that. That's got to mean something."

Corbin, the 24-year-old national champion of Barbados, had never played anybody quite like Phiona. After defeating her in Phiona's sixth game of the Olympiad, Corbin praised Phiona for playing so instinctively and "outside of the books." Books? Phiona had never opened a chess book. She didn't know what was *inside* the books.

Back at the hotel after the match, Corbin sought out Phiona and the two reviewed their game together move by move, breaking down the two minor blunders that cost Phiona the game. Corbin explained some tactics she used that Phiona had never seen before.

"Phiona has phenomenal potential for a fourteen-year-old," Corbin said. "I look forward to seeing her a few years from now. She looked like she was really beating herself up about this game. You see that in a player's eyes. You can see how competitive she is. She looks like she really has the heart of a champion."

On the shuttle bus from the hotel to the playing arena before Phiona's seventh and final game at the Chess Olympiad, Katende stared out the window into the Siberian mist and said, "Nobody here knows where this girl has come from. That God has picked this girl up from the slums in Katwe and has brought her to this place, it is not believable."

Phiona sat across the aisle lost in thought, but more resolute, older somehow than she seemed before any of her other six matches. Uganda's last match at the Olympiad was against Mozambique. Because Ivy was chosen to sit out the final match, Phiona was promoted to Board 1 for the first time in the tournament. She was pitted against 25-year-old Vania Fausto Da T. Vilhete, the Mozambique women's champion who was competing in her second Olympiad.

Playing more slowly, more deliberately, proving she'd learned from the previous games, Phiona eased into a positional advantage. The girl who on Day One did not understand anything about standard chess openings had clearly learned some of the nuances of a solid opening by the time she reached her final game. Phiona pressed her advantage throughout the middlegame until her opponent suddenly offered her a draw, essentially hoping to save face in a game that appeared to be a lost cause. Phiona's initial reaction was to keep playing, to finish her opponent off, but Katende leaned in to Phiona and whispered that because Uganda had already won two games and drawn the other, thus clinching victory in the overall match against Mozambique, that accepting a draw would be the proper etiquette. After the game, Katende playfully patted Phiona's head as he often does and joked, "Don't think you are a Board 1 player now."

Afterward Vilhete said, "My opponent is a very solid player. With help she can be a Grandmaster. I was fortunate to get a draw. I never saw any sign in her that she was only fourteen. The children of today grow up too fast."

Phiona's diary entries abruptly stopped after her second game at the Olympiad. She was too upset to write. She didn't even want her mother to know what she was feeling. Eleven days passed before she would pull out her diary again. Finally, on the team's last night in Khanty-Mansiysk, Phiona opened her diary and wrote one final entry from the Olympiad:

Dear mum,

I prayed my games very bad because I didn't know opens. I think that is why I was beaten. But there's a game I prayed I prayed very well and I thought I am going to wine. but they won me at the end. I was very disapointed and I went back to the hotel and I cried.

My feelings about the last game.

When we were going to pray the last game I was scared. What maked me to be so scared was the country I was playing. Although it is African country but I was scared because this time I was playing board one. Board one is where you find strong players from every country. I didn't want to take break fast because I new that Iam meeting strong player any time. So I went back to the room to prepare my self. What I knew that I was not going to lose that game. We were playing against mosbique. So when I riched the playing hall I prayed to God so that I could pray well. So the games started. The girl was play very quickly but me I was playing slowly. The time riched when I was wining the girl, so she had to think a lot. After asmall time the girl baged me adraw so I had to ask my coach weather he can accept me to make adraw. I made adraw. But when I finished my team mates told that I was wining because I had abetter position.

So after agame we went to the museum we so things of long ago. we saw some guns and we saw bones of big mammals and I was very happy to see all of that because I have never gone to the museum so this was my first time.

After that we went to the closing celemony. It was big inside. Down there was abig board. I saw some pieces on it. But they were not pieces they were people. But they were wearing things like pieces they were very nice. avery thing was organised very well. When they started giving trofys I was jelus and I cried. I was very disapointed and when the closing celemony ended we went to the last party.

At that time very tired and disapointed. I took some drinks and some eats. After that I had to live the place to go to the hotel. So I went with my coach but we left our team mates to continue these drinks. And I came back to pack my cloth. Because the following day we were going back home.

They stayed up late, night after night after night, the three siblings, Brian, Richard and Phiona, lying beside each other on the mattress on the floor of their pitch-dark shack in Katwe. Each night Phiona told her brothers a new and wondrous bedtime story that often held them rapt until dawn. One night she told them about the glittering, gleaming airport in a place called Dubai and how if you had some money you could buy anything you could ever imagine without ever leaving the terminal, including a beautiful blue car that for some reason had no roof on it. She told them about the cold white flakes that fall from the sky like rain. She told them about how somebody had told her that there are places in Russia where some days the sun never comes up and others when night never comes. She told them about the strange taste of Irish potatoes and about people who wear wires on their teeth to make them straight. She told them about meeting Garry Kasparov, the former world champion, and how he actually wanted to know her name. She told them about the day when the Ugandan team was walking around the city and people kept stopping them, asking to take their photo.

"Why did those people want to take pictures of you?" Brian asked.

"Because of our color," Phiona said.

Then Brian asked her, "You mean that those people in Russia, they have not seen soccer players who are black? Does that mean there are no black people on the other side of the world?"

"Those people think that for us to get this color we just paint it on ourselves," Phiona said. "They think that we really look just like them, but we wake up in the morning and we paint ourselves before we go out."

The morning after she flew home from Siberia, Phiona returned to Universal Junior Primary School to a hero's welcome. The headmaster had planned to hire a car to drive her to school from her home, but for lack of funds, they could only afford to ride the last 500 meters from the corner petrol station. Students and teachers lined the rutted dirt road that leads into the school's compound. Phiona arrived to hear fellow students chanting her name, *Phi-o-na! Phi-o-na!* and holding up handmade posters, one of which read, LONG LIVE UGANDA, LONG LIVE UNIVERSAL JUNIOR, LONG LIVE PHIONA MUTESI, FOR GOD AND OUR COUNTRY.

Phiona said a few words and then distributed to her schoolmates some candies that she'd bought in the airport the day before with an allowance that all players received at the Olympiad. She would use much of that stipend to pay off her mother's debts, including back rent and money Harriet owed to suppliers at the Kibuye market. The little that was left over Phiona used to buy hair extensions, a teenage indulgence she had never heard of before going to Russia.

Once again Phiona felt profoundly affected by her time outside of Katwe. "Surely, the way I think really changed," Phiona says. "All along, all I knew was Africa. When I went to Russia my mind was broadened. I realized that another place was better than ours. I noted the way they behaved, what they feed on, the kind of lifestyle they lead, and they are totally different from ours here. Actually, that motivates me. Because if I'm in this kind of life and I see another person who is in a better state, then I get a sense that perhaps if I work hard I can also be able to achieve what other people are having as a better life."

Phiona has learned to sense the lessons on her own that Katende once needed to fill in for her.

"I will never forget how I lost the first Olympiad games," Phiona says. "I won't forget because some games I played badly and I made terrible mistakes. I learned from that. The way I played the first games was not the same way I played the games at the end. I have learned some of the openings and even the endgames and I can now play them much better. The Olympiad was so challenging. It has given me great power to work hard and practice so that the next time I go to an Olympiad I can win the games that I lost and then someday become a Grandmaster."

When she is asked how long becoming a Grandmaster might take, she is confused. That sort of specific time frame question makes no sense to a kid from Katwe who never plans beyond the end of the day. Any goal is "just there."

Finally, Phiona replied, "How can I know when what will be will be?"

Endgame

Chapter 10
Hurdles

Phiona Mutesi's older sister Night *(left)* and mother Harriet
Nakku sell vegetables at Kampala's Kibuye Market, the life for
which Phiona appeared destined until she discovered chess.

He couldn't win. John Akii-Bua was not supposed to win. One of 43 children from his father's nine wives, Akii-Bua was born in 1949 and grew up in Lira, a small village in northern Uganda, where he struggled for one meal a day that he often had to hunt down in the bush. He dropped out of school when his father died and came to Kampala in his late teens seeking a better life. He found a job as a policeman, discovered competitive running while training for the police force, and joined the police track team. His training regime was rudimentary, partly because there was no modern athletic track in all of Uganda. Akii-Bua became a 400-meter hurdler, but unlike other runners who carefully plotted their steps between hurdles and always led with the same leg, Akii-Bua jumped the hurdles in however many steps were necessary to travel from one to the next and led with whichever leg happened to be closest to the hurdle at the time. The 23-year-old Akii-Bua was not a favorite at the 1972 Olympics because he lacked the proper experience in international competition. He was running the Olympic final from Lane 1, the last lane he would have chosen. Above all he was from Uganda. Ugandans don't win.

When Akii-Bua left the starting blocks at Munich's Olympic Stadium on September 2, 1972, hardly anybody in Uganda even knew who he was. A mere 47.82 seconds later, Akii-Bua was a national hero. Akii-Bua won the 400-meter hurdles, hunting down his rivals and then leaving them behind to stare at the bottom of his two-year-old track shoes, one of which, according to legend, was missing a spike. Akii-Bua set a new world record and captured Uganda's first Olympic gold medal. After the race, he joyously jogged a victory lap with a flag unfurled above his head, beginning a tradition at track events that endures to this day.

Very few Ugandans were able to watch Akii-Bua's race on television, but shortly after the race was over, Radio Uganda blared the news across the country.

"Uganda's athletics fraternity was following John and could see the progress in him, but the whole country did not know much about athletics because as a sport it was not known like football," says Daniel Tamwesigire, another 400-meter hurdler who became Akii-Bua's teammate shortly after the Olympics. "You could look at the seeding in terms of the lanes and it was not the lane you expect for a winner. The rest of the world was not expecting a medal for him. John told me later that his attitude was, 'Hey, I have nothing to lose here. Let me go and see what can I achieve.'"

Three days after the race, 11 Israeli athletes and coaches were killed by Palestinian terrorists and the world quickly forgot Akii-Bua, but Uganda's president Idi Amin made certain his country remained focused on its new conquering hero. When Akii-Bua returned to his country he was personally received by Amin. He was promoted in the police force. A house was built for him in one of the finest neighborhoods in Kampala. Even a major thoroughfare in the capital city was renamed Akii-Bua Road. Plans were announced for the construction of John Akii-Bua Stadium. Akii-Bua's stunning victory had provided a ray of hope for all Ugandans that success on that type of grand international stage was actually possible.

"John was a great role model," Tamwesigire says. "He loved to encourage his peers and those athletes lower than him in stature, which is not common among top athletes. His achievement would inspire all Ugandans that followed him to dream bigger."

In the ensuing years, Akii-Bua struggled to recapture the moment, though he was still among the 400-meter hurdles favorites leading up to the 1976 Olympics in Montreal—until the African nations chose to boycott those Olympics right before the Games began.

While many members of Akii-Bua's tribe were being murdered during the bloody years of the Amin regime, Akii-Bua was protected by his fame, though several attempts were made to evict his family from the house that Amin had built for him. When the regime collapsed in 1979, Akii-Bua fled to Kenya for fear of being jailed as a collaborator, despite the fact that three of his brothers had been murdered by Amin's forces. In Kenya, Akii-Bua was forced into a refugee camp, from which he and his family were rescued by his shoe sponsor and brought to Germany for several years before he eventually returned to Uganda and his job with the police.

Akii-Bua died in 1997 at the age of 47 as a man of modest means and modest celebrity. Only in death was he properly remembered for his accomplishments. His body lay in state in Uganda's parliament and his funeral was a national event.

"As a sports hero John died when he was still very young and the country definitely needed him," Tamwesigire says. "His contemporaries in other countries are still alive and playing a big role in developing gold medalists in those countries. John would have been a leader in our Olympic movement, but his demise denies our country that type of advantage. He should still be here telling his story about winning the gold medal to young people to inspire them."

However, Akii-Bua does live on in the Ugandan schoolyards, on the tongues of young runners who invoke his name while sometimes having no idea who he is.

"When John won the gold medal, people in Uganda replaced the word 'running' with 'Akii-Bua,'" Tamwesigire says. "So even today you'll hear kids say that some boy '*akii-buas*,' meaning he 'runs.' That is his legacy."

Could she win? Ugandan women don't win, do they? Plenty of Ugandan men believe that women shouldn't even compete in sports. But both of Dorcus Inzikuru's parents were runners, father and mother, and they told their daughter often about a certain magical day in Munich. Inzikuru grew up idolizing Akii-Bua, who won his gold medal ten years before Inzikuru was born in the tiny town of Vurra in Arua district, tucked into the northwest corner of Uganda near the Sudanese border. Inzikuru was the oldest of six girls in her family. Both of her older brothers died in childhood.

Inzikuru's family was so poor that when she ran in school track meets, she did so barefooted. She couldn't afford running shoes. She won anyway, jumping out to early leads and never looking back, the tiny girl seeming to dance across the ground like a sprite, dominating all of her local competition until as a teenager she was spotted and brought to Kampala to train, like so many others dreaming of a better life.

She eventually had to leave Uganda for Italy because her home country simply didn't have the training facilities, the coaching, or the competitors necessary to prepare her for elite competition. Inzikuru began her career as a 5,000-meter runner, but that race proved a little too long for her. Then one day in 2003 her coach suggested she try her sport's most unusual race, the 3,000-meter steeplechase, an event that features five hurdles, including one with a water jump—all the deterrents that track has to offer. Inzikuru decided that she kind of enjoyed getting wet.

The 3,000-meter steeplechase would be contested for the first time ever at a World Championship during the 2005 meet in Helsinki, Finland, and while most of the athletics community didn't realize it yet, Inzikuru was among the best in the world. She was an unknown. Her name was misspelled on her passport and every story written about her dashing her way into the 3,000-meter steeplechase final perpetuated the error. Inzikuru didn't care. Her surname, Inzikuru, translates to "no respect."

Daniel Tamwesigire, at that time the president of the Uganda Athletics Federation, pinned Inzikuru's number to her chest before the gold-medal race and then asked her, "What are you going to do?"

"I am going to leave them," Inzikuru said.

When Inzikuru left the starting line at Helsinki's Olympic Stadium on August 8, 2005, many people across Uganda were just learning for the first time who she was. A little more than nine minutes later, Dorcus Inzikuru was a national hero.

"The race was playing in all of the bars where they usually watch football," Godfrey Gali says. "People stood up on their seats. People were shouting. Tension was so high. People all over Kampala were watching the race with great anticipation."

Tamwesigire believes he may have been the most nervous person inside the stadium that day.

"When you are the president of the Federation, you can't sit," Tamwesigire says. "I had brought our national flag, but I left it on my seat and moved closer to the track. When Inzikuru won the race, I was looking for this flag to give to her, but I couldn't find it anywhere. Watching the race was very exciting. She was a very good distance ahead of the pack. She left them."

Preferring to pace the field, Inzikuru ran in front for the entire race, winning in a time 9:18.24, more than two seconds clear of the field. Inzikuru jogged her victory lap without a flag after winning Uganda's first international gold medal in any sport since her idol, Akii-Bua, 33 years before, thus joining him as only the second sports role model ever produced by their nation. By contrast, the United States has won more than 1,000 gold medals just in its Olympic history, and Uganda's neighbor Kenya has won 23 Olympic gold medals.

"When it came time for the medal award, Inzikuru was crying instead of smiling because she couldn't believe what she had done," Tamwesigire says. "She couldn't believe that the national anthem being played was for her. I didn't expect the level of excitement and knowledge back at home. People called me asking when her flight was coming back so the celebration could begin. I said, 'What? The lady is going somewhere first to continue her training.' They said, 'No, she must come here first.'"

The Ugandan government chartered a plane to bring Inzikuru home. A jubilant crowd of 10,000 people met her at the airport in Entebbe. The following morning a motorcade of 12 motorcycles followed by a Mercedes-Benz convertible carrying Inzikuru required five hours to carry her the 30 kilometers from Entebbe to Kampala as euphoric Ugandans lined up along the roadside. One elated young man ran the entire route beside Inzikuru's car. After touring all of the major streets of Kampala to more cheering crowds, Inzikuru was honored in a special session convened by Uganda's parliament and invited for dinner with the president.

"Inzikuru has become a national hero known all over, just like Akii-Bua," Gali says. "In schools now when they are teaching mathematics, they say, 'If Inzikuru is running 10 kilometers per hour and she must run 50 kilometers, how long will it take Inzikuru to cover that distance?'"

Inzikuru would become known as "the Gazelle of Arua." After winning the 3,000-meter steeplechase in the 2006 Commonwealth Games, she was slowed by injuries. Then she became pregnant and, after missing two years following the birth of her child, she has only recently begun to train again at an elite level.

"For many years Ugandan society was not positive about women in sport because they thought sport is masculine and while top sportswomen might be admired as great athletes, they were not admired as great family people because they were off the expected road," Tamwesigire says. "Inzikuru has helped change that. People are proud of this lady. Because of Inzikuru, Ugandans are no longer saying that sport is not a woman thing."

"Inzikuru has inspired and motivated so many women," says Jasper Aligawesa, the general secretary of Uganda's National Council of Sports. "When she won the medal every school wanted to invite her there to show kids that you can come from a very poor background and if you put in good effort you can still become a champion. Inzikuru has become synonymous with the word 'champion.' She may be a tiny woman but every Ugandan looks up to her."

She could win. Inzikuru helped her believe. Phiona Mutesi hasn't heard of all that much, but she has heard of Inzikuru. Everybody in Uganda has heard of the Gazelle of Arua. Phiona knows Inzikuru is the best female athlete in her country and she knows that they both began from nowhere with nothing and no respect.

"I know that she runs for Uganda and she's a world champion," Phiona says. "Inzikuru actually motivates me because I know she has gone through the same lifestyle I have gone through and so whenever I look at her I feel like I am encouraged. That I can also make it."

Phiona thought of Inzikuru on the eve of the Rwabushenyi Memorial Chess Championship staged in December of 2010 at the Lugogo Sports Complex in Kampala. All of the top Ugandan players were there. Seven games in three grueling days. After returning to the Katwe chess project from the Olympiad with a new level of confidence forged by competing day after day against the world's elite players, the annual Rwabushenyi tournament, one of the most coveted titles in Ugandan chess, would be Phiona's first opportunity to show how much her game had grown from her experience in Russia.

"I did not think I could become the champion at that event," Phiona says, "because all of the big ladies were there and they were telling me how they'd been training using their computers and personally I was just training with my friends in the project."

After winning her first-round game, Phiona found herself staring across the board in the second game at her Olympiad teammate Rita Nsubuga.

"Whenever I play Phiona I really focus because I have this fear in me about how will I resign to this young girl," Rita says. "I remember I was winning that game. I really focused and I had the game in my hands and she saw it."

Phiona admits she fell into a weak position against Rita and was on the verge of surrendering. "I remember that right from the start Rita was having an upper hand," Phiona says. "In the middle of the game I had no position whatsoever and actually I lost hope. I stood up and I had a chance to look at other games of other project children who were also taking part in the tournament and I saw some of them were also having very terrible positions, but we had agreed that this time we were going to compete and not just participate. So I sat down and I endured to continue to think and play and luckily enough the game turned to my advantage."

Says Rita, "I touched on a piece that I was not supposed to move, but by the rules I had to move it, and so Phiona ended up winning. I made a lot of blunders. So she ended up taking the game and she was so excited. I was so hurt, because it was my game. I felt so bad. It was so painful."

Later that afternoon, Phiona found herself facing Ivy Claire Amoko, her Board 1 teammate at the Olympiad, considered the country's national champion. Phiona was intimidated from the start. She again had thoughts of resigning early in the game. "She was winning right from the opening, so why would she resign?" Ivy says incredulously. "I was so beaten that I couldn't even understand where I went wrong. She beat me so badly I felt like I had not played in ten years."

The following morning Phiona faced Goretti Angolikin, another strong player whom Phiona had feared playing in the past. But whether or not Phiona knew it, she was not the only apprehensive player at the board. "To be honest, I was scared of her," Goretti says. "Phiona has a coach. She does more training than I do. I just had a feeling she would win. In chess, once you're scared, it's hard to get a good result."

Still, Goretti got off to a fast start and familiar doubts began to creep into Phiona's mind. "When I saw Coach Robert coming to look at my game I remembered how he had given us a caution never to resign, so when I saw him I feared to resign," Phiona says. "When I remembered that agreement, it somehow encouraged me and I just said, 'Okay, let me continue.'"

As Phiona and Goretti reached the endgame, the contest appeared destined for a draw. But Goretti made one small blunder and Phiona recognized it immediately and stole the game. It would be Goretti's only loss of the tournament.

At this point in the event, it occurred to Katende that Phiona was playing the best chess of her life and that if she finished strong in her final three matches she could well be the women's champion, but he chose not to share his thoughts with her. He knew that Phiona never thinks that way, never thinks ahead, and it could be perilous to plant that idea in her mind.

In her next game, Phiona faced Grace Kigeni. "I remember she beat me easily, which was quite embarrassing," Grace says. "She played so well that I remember thinking, 'This girl is becoming such a strong and confident player. This girl is not the same girl who played at the Olympiad.'"

Later that evening, Phiona easily defeated Joan Nakimuli for her sixth straight win. Phiona wasn't aware that her victory in that game secured the tournament championship until all of the matches in that round had been completed. When Katende informed her of the news, Phiona's reaction was typically reserved, at least until Ivan, Benjamin, Samuel, and many of the other competitors from Katwe came to congratulate her and coaxed a shy smile. A win for anybody from Katende's project has always been treated as a victory for everybody, dating all the way back to the days of The Children's Team. Katende says he couldn't truly gauge Phiona's joy until she walked out of the playing hall with a subtle bounce in her step that he had noticed before following significant victories.

Even after clinching the Rwabushenyi championship, there was still one challenge remaining for Phiona. In the final round, she was slated to face Christine Namaganda, the same girl from whom Katende had once drawn inspiration to train his own champion. Katende had never shared that story with Phiona, but Phiona was aware of Christine's championship pedigree, and before the game she came to Katende and told him, "Coach, I am nervous. That Christine is tough and she is experienced."

Katende tried to comfort Phiona. He reminded her that she had played against more talented players at the Olympiad. Then moments before the game was to begin, Christine approached Phiona and asked her if she would accept a draw, admitting she was reluctant to compete against Phiona after seeing how well she had played in the tournament to that point. Phiona consulted Katende, who insisted that she play for the experience but told her that because she did not need to win to be the tournament champion, she could accept a draw during the game. Phiona quickly jumped ahead of Christine with a strong opening and when Christine requested a draw early in the middlegame, Phiona granted it to help Christine save face. Suddenly there was nobody left to fear.

"A young girl like her shouldn't be able to win that tournament," Rita says. "But all of us made blunders against her and she took advantage of us. When you look at Phiona's background, she is totally different from the rest of us, so you have to feel happy for her when she wins."

"Maybe some people were surprised she won that tournament because she was so young, but those of us who know her were not shocked," Grace says. "She deserved it."

For the first time, Phiona was the undisputed best women's chess player in all of Uganda. For the first time, she was beginning to leave them.

The first 13 years of her life, she was somebody else. She was Fiona. Because her name was never formally spelled out for her, when Harriet's daughter began to learn to write in primary school, she spelled her name the way it sounded to her: F-I-O-N-A. When she reached P4, she met another student who shared her name, but spelled it P-H-I-O-N-A. She didn't really understand how their names could be spelled differently, so she kept using "Fiona" until the day she looked at her passport to travel to the chess tournament in Sudan. During the passport application process, Godfrey Gali filled out her documents without bothering to check how she spelled her name. Gali knew a woman with that name who spelled it "Phiona," so that is how he printed it on the application. When Fiona received the passport, she noticed the alternate spelling. Katende told her that from that point on she must begin spelling her name with a "Ph" or risk bureaucratic hassles whenever she used her passport for identification. And so Fiona became Phiona, through no choice of her own.

Phiona isn't Fiona. Less so every day.

Rodney Suddith remembers the first time he ever crossed paths with the girl back in 2006. He visited the chess project and asked Katende to point out some of the children who were rising above the others with their skill level. At that time, 10-year-old Phiona had been out of school for most of the last six years. She spoke Luganda but could neither read nor write in that language. She could not speak any English, could write only her name and a handful of other words, and could understand just the simplest phrases.

"The first time I met Phiona I think I may have glimpsed her face, but I basically just saw the top of her head because she wouldn't make eye contact," Suddith says. "Robert translated, so I'm assuming Phiona said something, but I never heard it. I was really taken by what an extreme introvert she was. She would answer a very direct question, but never with more than the most simple answer to get the conversation over. Unlike a lot of Ugandans who like a physical touch, a pat on the shoulder, she seemed to shy away from that as well. But each visit after that, I watched her progress and grow in confidence, not only in chess, but in life."

From the beginning, Suddith also noticed Phiona's compassion for the other kids. Each day when she arrived at the project she would tend to many of the younger children. While most her peers would move straight for the chessboards and begin playing, Phiona would first make sure certain kids she was looking out for were there and often sat with them to help teach them how to play. She always volunteered to prepare the porridge and when she didn't cook, she was always appreciative of those who did. Following Katende's advice, Phiona never left the project without thanking everybody who had helped out that day.

Suddith could see himself in this girl. Phiona was another kid whose life had left its predestined path through sport. Another grinder who has lived the in-between. Another person from a sheltered background inspired by the idea that there might be something else out there. He particularly remembers the day when Phiona returned from Sudan with a different level of self-confidence.

"There was a newfound spark there and that comes from being competitive," Suddith says. "I asked her, 'Did you enjoy your trip?' Phiona told me, 'Yes, we won.' That wasn't even my question, but I liked her answer."

By that time, Phiona had embraced chess as her true calling. "I love chess with all of my heart," Phiona says. "And when you love something with all your heart, it brings many other things. I wouldn't have gone out of the country if it wasn't for playing chess. I wasn't schooling, but I began schooling again because of chess. I wouldn't have met Coach Robert and so many other people if it wasn't for chess. Because of the love I have for chess I am able to access all that."

"If you're a slum kid your personality is suffocated by the need to survive," Suddith says. "But what is so rare about Phiona as a kid in Katwe is that she doesn't ignore what's around her. She observes it and she absorbs it and she learns from it. And as she's seen some of the horror stories that are part of daily life in the slum, it strikes a deeper chord with Phiona than in her peers. It touches her. She's very sensitive to what other people are thinking and feeling and I think that plays well with her chess."

Katende attributes much of Phiona's personal transformation to the fact that she has found religion. "It is really hard to measure spiritual aspects because there are no parameters," Katende says. "You cannot really know whether the wind is blowing unless you see it shaking things. You need to see its effect. I can confidently say that Phiona was not good spiritually because of the way she used to quarrel and say vulgar things to the other children. But I would say that she has made a complete U-turn. Her conduct is totally different from the way she was before she joined the program. She has even developed grace in her."

Phiona worships every day either at a church near her school or at her mother's church closer to their home. One of Phiona's few regular possessions is a tiny dog-eared Bible that she carries with her almost everywhere she goes. She believes in God, even as she is still figuring out the impact religion can have on her life.

"Getting saved has really helped me greatly because sometimes I can have problems and I just put them in prayer requests and I've seen God able to rescue us," Phiona says. "I remember one time when I fell sick and I was almost dying and there was a certain pastor who came and made me confess some words and after confessing those words the following day I felt like I was getting better. In the days that followed I got healed, so I understand that being a born-again Christian has helped me a lot. I appreciate that God has helped me stay alive."

In January of 2011, Phiona's story was published in *ESPN The Magazine*. Until that point, Phiona's exploits were known only to those at the chess project and inside Sports Outreach. Though chess is not among the sports most closely followed in Uganda, suddenly the nation began to discover the prodigy in its midst.

When the story was published, Uganda's National Council of Sports increased its organization's annual funding for chess from two million to five million shillings and pledged even more support for the sport in the future.

Says Godfrey Gali, "That story caused our local media to say, 'Who is this person? We didn't know.' They came to me asking for interviews. Also, from the international media, they came around as well. It has opened up Phiona's story to the world. Our administrators in the ministry of sport, they were all asking me, 'Who is this kid? When did this happen? How did this happen? We had no idea this sport was this popular.'"

"Chess tends to be a sport that is mostly hidden indoors," says Daniel Tamwesigire, who is now Uganda's Commissioner for Physical Education and Sports. "The spectator population is very small. It is not a major story in our newspapers. But Phiona can make it so. What she needs is exposure. If the press picks up on chess as regular publicity material, the community will come to know, the schools will come to know, the young girls will come to know. We don't have a very good reading culture so we also need the electronic media, the radios and the televisions, to talk about this young lady. We just need to figure out how to focus the camera on her in Uganda. Then she can make a difference."

"Phiona's story reminds me of another teenage girl from nowhere," says Jasper Aligawesa. "I believe that Phiona could be another Inzikuru. If this girl goes to an international competition and wins a gold medal, she could have the same impact, because don't forget that track is not as popular as football. When we hold a track event in Uganda the entrance is free, but we don't see people. But when Inzikuru won a gold medal then everyone was in the streets. If you ask anybody, 'Who is Inzikuru?' they say, 'The Gazelle of Arua.' Someday maybe when you ask, 'Who is Phiona?' they will say, 'The Queen of Katwe.'"

Teopista Agutu was surfing online in the spring of 2011 when she stumbled upon an article in London's *Guardian* newspaper about Phiona Mutesi, a follow-up to the *ESPN* story. Agutu, who lives with her husband and two sons in one of Kampala's affluent gated communities known as Naalya Estates, phoned the city's daily newspaper, *New Vision*, and asked whether anyone there had heard of Phiona. *New Vision* had begun following Phiona's career and so one of the reporters gave Agutu a phone number for Robert Katende. She phoned Katende and told him she had always wanted her sons, 10-year-old Stefan and seven-year-old Samuel, to learn chess and asked if Phiona would be interested in tutoring them. Agutu offered to bring her children to Katwe, but because they had never been there before, Katende felt that Phiona should go to Agutu's home so that Phiona would not be embarrassed—and her teaching potentially compromised—by her students' finding out where she lives.

A week later, during a school holiday, Phiona boarded a taxi for the seven-kilometer ride to another world. She walked into a home with a brand-new flat-screen television, children's bedrooms the same size as her shack, and a sparkling clean toilet with Mickey Mouse stickers over the commode. There was a treehouse in the yard from which one could get a panoramic view of Kampala that did not include the lowlands of Katwe.

"Normally a community like Naalya would not allow a slum kid through the gate," Katende says, "but Phiona has developed a certain kind of potential that opens up a door."

"Phiona has a skill we value," Agutu says. "It's all about what she knows and not who she is or where she comes from."

As many as a dozen kids from the Naalya neighborhood show up on school holidays to meet Phiona and several other children from the chess project anxious to make the journey out of Katwe. They are paid only for their travel expenses.

Phiona began teaching chess with the pawn. Then the rook. Then the bishop, just as she had once learned from Gloria and Gloria had once learned from Benjamin and Benjamin from Ivan and Ivan from Katende himself. The curriculum is the same. In fact, Stefan executed the Fool's Mate on Samuel several times before Phiona taught Samuel how to combat it.

"Phiona was telling us about how she went to Sudan and Russia and she was playing chess and beating people from all over the world and I was amazed," Stefan says. "I was wondering, 'How could that happen?' She made very many articles in the newspapers until she became a very popular person in Uganda. Coming from where she comes from, it inspires me. I know she is the best player among girls in Uganda and that is a good teacher to have."

Phiona has also created her own informal chess project at her secondary school, tutoring 20 of her fellow female students in the game. Chess has become so popular that Phiona's teacher, Abbey Ssentogo, has often had to confiscate chessboards from students who are surreptitiously playing the game during class.

"What I know about Phiona is that she's influential because when she started playing chess in school the number of girls playing started increasing every day," Ssentogo says. "They know that chess has taken Phiona to different countries. Many kids are getting interested because of that. Sometimes kids when they hear about something good happening to somebody they get encouraged. They are proud of her."

International publicity has also led Phiona to acquire pen pals around the world, including an American convict named Damion Coppedge, who is serving time for manslaughter at the Wende Correctional Facility in Alden, New York. Coppedge read Phiona's story and the two began a chess game through the mail. Coppedge has sent Phiona three chess books, a check for $25 that prompted Katende to open Phiona's first bank account, and the following note:

Dear Phiona,

 I write to you happy to hear from you & your coach. I thought I would never get a letter back, and when I did I smiled with excitement.

 Your letter was the very first one I ever received from my original home. I write to you and Robert not only as a fellow student of chess, but also a brother in a distant land. Captured long ago were my ancestors and as I descend from them I'm delighted to reconnect with you as a friend and brother. I thank you for agreeing to play with me. I absolutely love everything about chess. I have a small library of chess books in my cell along with 2 chess sets made of plastic. My father taught me to play when I was 8 years old. I've been hooked since. I am 34 and I don't have much competition here in this prison.

 Don't worry about me defeating you. I read that you make everybody's pieces retreat until there is nothing for them to do but resign!

 I have 6½ years to come out of this place. I've been in here since 1997. When I was younger I was living without good in my life and I killed my best friend by playing with a loaded gun which went off & hit him & took his life.

 Every day I wish I could bring him back. Every day I wish I could change the past. Every day I escape my wishes through an intricate maze of chess, prayer and deep thought. The prison life is like a chess game with many dimensions. Every day is an obstacle & challenge. A temptation to explode and attack. But like in chess sometimes restraint is better for your position than to attack. In prison the best position is to be walking out of the place and going home never to come back. So I work hard to restrain myself, not involving myself in nonsense. My king (ME) remains mostly castled (in my cell) and away from the center of the board where many empty-minded pawns roam.

Thank you very much for reaching out.

Take care, Damion

Phiona says that she can relate to Coppedge. Both are bound by tragic circumstances, both struggling to survive against the odds of their environment. Katende believes that Phiona is just beginning to realize the positive influence her life story can have on other people's lives.

"I want to say that Phiona understands what she's accomplished because she compares how she is with how she was," Katende says. "She was really proud to complete primary school. She is proud to begin speaking some English. Even when she's going through trauma and being at school with nothing, she still has that self-esteem. Other students don't come to her directly, but they know what she's done. They whisper, 'Oh, that's the girl.' In a way it gives her confidence. She may not have enough money to visit the canteen, but they look at her as though she is a hero. Still, according to the way she sees herself, she has not done what she wants to do. She is really still striving. All the time."

"I don't feel like I'm the best woman chess player in the country," Phiona says. "I realize thinking that could hold me back. The moment I feel like I'm the best, then I won't be able to add on, so I don't even in any way get close to that. I always work as though I'm not the one who is the champion and then I am able to continue to train."

Katwe is not a place where people trumpet their own success. Those instances are rare and thus can attract unwanted attention. Any personal celebration is best kept private. When Phiona was preparing to begin P7 in 2010, she had to fill out some forms that included her date of birth. She asked her mother. She asked Brian. Of course, nobody knew what to tell her. She wanted to fill in something, so she wrote March 28, simply because in P5 her English teacher had organized a party for her class on March 28, so Phiona chose that day as her birthday. "I had a happy memory of that day, so that is my birthday now," Phiona says. "On that day in 2011 when I turned fifteen I was at home on holiday and I called out to the children in my neighborhood and I gave them sweets. That is how I celebrated. I did that because I wanted it to be a special day."

Yet for all the positives that chess has brought to her life, Phiona still suffers just as Fiona once did. When Phiona returned from the Chess Olympiad in October of 2010, she discovered that her family had been evicted from their home again. Harriet was two months behind on the rent payments and when the landlord discovered that mzungu from America had visited Harriet's shack with their notepads and cameras, the landlord believed that Harriet must have some money. When Harriet insisted she did not, the family was tossed out. With money from the stipend that Phiona was allotted at the Olympiad, the family was able to relocate to another shack.

Phiona is in boarding school at St. Mbuga Secondary School through the Popp Scholarship and lives at home only during the holidays. She is reminded every day by the hunger that often grips her gut and the rotten stench that permeates the school compound that some things have not changed. She is still a slum kid in Katwe, constantly confronted by an environment that conspires against her on so many levels.

So many hurdles.

There is a well-known story in Uganda about a mzungu who watches a Ugandan man fishing in a lake. The Ugandan catches a fish, cooks it, and eats it while sitting under a shady tree. The mzungu asks him, "Why don't you catch more fish and sell them to make money?"

"Then what?" the Ugandan fisherman asks.

"You can use that money to start a business," the mzungu says.

"Then what?"

"You can use money from your business to build yourself a home."

"Then what?"

"You can become a rich man and relax."

"If the ultimate goal is to relax, then why should I go through all of that work?" the Ugandan says. "I am already relaxing now."

Phiona must defy Uganda, defy the sentiment that surrounds her, tugs at her, whether it be lethargy or hopelessness. She must defy the paradox of a country so fertile that many Ugandans spend their entire days chopping down tall grass that seems to grow almost as fast as it can be cut, but still struggles to properly feed its population. She must defy her country's rampant inflation, because Phiona's chess career needs sponsorship and so Uganda's economic future is tied to hers. For the first time, it actually matters to her what is going on beyond "just there."

Uganda's future lies in the hands of Yoweri Museveni, the man who once protected Katende and his grandmother in the bush of the Luwero Triangle and then became president. Like all Ugandan presidents, Museveni, the former rebel, is dogged by rebels. Uganda is a nation struggling with a lingering civil war that compelled the United States to send special advisers to the country in 2011 to help the Ugandan military hunt down Joseph Kony and his Lord's Resistance Army and bring them to justice for the atrocities they have committed over the last 25 years.

"Sometimes it makes me want to shed tears when I think of our future in Uganda," Katende says. "That's why I invest my life in the children. The only way to break the chain of poverty is to do it with the children. It is too late for the adults. We have to let that generation go and start from here."

Because Uganda's economy has still yet to recover from the damage done by Amin and his successors, both John Akii-Bua and Dorcus Inzikuru often had to leave the country to train in places with more modern facilities. It is galling to Ugandans that a neighboring country like Kenya collects gold medals routinely in international competition, yet Akii-Bua and Inzikuru are the only gold medal winners in any sport in Uganda's history. Ugandans revere soccer above all other sports, yet the country has never qualified for the World Cup. It is a nation so starved for recognition on the world stage that many of its people have begun to long for the time of Idi Amin, whose megalomania pushed Uganda into the international consciousness both on and off the field.

"General Amin, among all the presidents that the country has ever had, promoted sport more than any other, although he is not known for that," Daniel Tamwesigire says. "In sports you realize that most of Uganda's achievements came in the 1970s, the reason being that we had stable physical education and a good follow-up system for athletes who performed well in sports. Comparing us with other African nations, at that point we were ahead, but there came a time when our systems were interfered with while the others continued, and we have never recovered."

"Our current president needs to be better educated on the issue so we can get more funding," Godfrey Gali says. "To Museveni sports is nothing more than leisure. A pastime. I remember once he told us that Uganda must spend all of its money on roads and hospitals. Sports is not a priority for him. He has the wrong perspective of the contributions that sports could make to our national pride."

Because of lack of funding, Ugandan chess players rarely take part in tournaments outside of their own country. Even a tournament inside Uganda requires money for registration, transportation, and meals, which is often too much for the chess federation to underwrite on its own. In September of 2011 Phiona qualified to play in the All-Africa Games in Mozambique, but the funds never materialized to send her. Over the last two years, Phiona has had to turn down invitations from tournaments all over Africa, and even some inside Uganda, because the trips were too expensive. The Uganda Chess Federation could not even afford to stage its own national junior championship in 2010.

"Uganda used to be a force in chess inside Africa," says former national team coach Dr. George Zirembuzi. "There was a time when we were third on the continent with only Egypt and Tunisia ahead of us, but now Botswana and Zambia and Zimbabwe and South Africa have moved so fast ahead of us. They even have Grandmasters. We have really fallen behind."

"It is a struggle," says Joachim Okoth, Uganda's current national chess coach. "We lack facilities. We play our chess at an old tennis club. We have gotten the permission to take chess to the schools, but we don't have the equipment. We don't have the boards."

"The way we train our players in Uganda is crude and rudimentary," Gali says. "We don't have many coaches so our children will just play the game and someone will tell them what they think is a good move and what is not."

It makes sense that Uganda's two most celebrated athletes are runners. Hurdlers. That's what you do in Uganda, run until you reach the next hurdle. Dorh Aku-Bua and Inzikuru eventually had to run away from their country and the question remains whether Phiona, too, would have to somehow leave Uganda to reach her full potential in chess.

Uganda's best chess player is currently living in England. Stephen Kawuma is part of what is becoming his nation's lost generation of chess. Stephen's father, Medi, was one of the pioneers of the Uganda Chess Federation and taught his three sons to play the game. The Kawumas bought chess books for the boys to study, which was all Stephen needed to reach the top level of Ugandan chess. Stephen is a FIDE Master who has played in every Chess Olympiad since 2000, but has never performed as well as he would like. He evolved in the game by playing whatever competition was presented to him in Uganda along with games on the Internet. But like every Ugandan before him, he has never had a true coach. Many chess players believe that it takes a Grandmaster to make one, and there simply isn't access to that in Uganda.

"We have had a coach, Dr. Zirembuzi, who once trained in Russia, but he has given us everything he can," Stephen Kawuma says. "To reach the next level we need a Grandmaster or an International Master who could sit down and analyze our games and give us the needed boost. For so many years, Uganda's top players have done their own work. Today I read this book. Tomorrow another book. You have knowledge, but that's haphazard knowledge and that doesn't help against the world's top players. I'm twenty-nine and my game is the same as it was ten years ago."

Stephen works as a refrigeration engineer in Southampton, England. Without any sponsorship money, chess has become more of a hobby, just a small part of his life. He could train with a chess coach 75 miles away in London, but that would cost 50 pounds an hour. There is an American Grandmaster offering him coaching online, but Stephen has to consider the endgame. How long can he continue to invest energy and money in chess?

"Chess demands a lot of time," Stephen says. "I got to a point where there was no time for chess. Now I'm married and from observation, when you get married your chess goes down. I don't regret that. I'm happy to be married and to have a job."

While FIDE Master is the highest ranking ever achieved by any Ugandan, Stephen says he would need to reach the next level, International Master, to start potentially receiving a regular stipend to play in tournaments. He rarely plays in FIDE-rated tournaments other than the Olympiad. He does play in club tournaments, but they do nothing to help his rating. He is close to a level where he could sustain himself as a chess player, but he has begun to question whether he has the drive and the resources to keep climbing.

Stephen's older brother, Moses, was once Uganda's best player, but he also left Uganda for England. Moses also achieved the rating of FIDE Master before reaching a point where he could sense his dream of becoming a Grandmaster was no longer possible and he basically retired from the sport, playing only recreational online chess. He has offered to be Stephen's coach, but Moses cannot take his brother to greater heights.

Stephen's younger brother, Patrick, is 20 years old and benefits from the road map provided by his older brothers. They supply him with the books and the computer software that he needs to reach their level. Stephen believes that Patrick, who ranks one rung below his brothers as a Candidate Master, is already capable of playing at his level and believes that in a few years Patrick could be an International Master if only he could find the proper coaching and competition.

"When our best players leave the country that's a brain drain for Ugandan chess," says Stephen Kisuze, vice chairman of the Uganda Chess Federation. "Because there is so little funding to travel to tournaments outside the country we must count on our own players to make each other better."

There are only two tournaments staged each year for national team players in Uganda, far fewer than most countries with a chess federation. Ugandan chess players are a family and they gather often in Kampala to play in the national league, but they are no longer able to push each other to become better in the game because they all know each other's tactics too well. Their regular competition is with club teams, the Mulago Kings and the Mulago Queens, which comprise many of the 2010 Olympiad participants, and is staged at Kampala's upscale Hotel Africana, where during breaks between games Phiona and the other players gaze curiously at the vast swimming pool that occupies the courtyard.

Harold Wanyama, who played Board 1 at the 2010 Olympiad and is the top player still living in Uganda, admits that he has become complacent because there isn't enough competition in his country to challenge him. He has twice missed out after qualifying for the Olympiad because Uganda could not afford to send him and he says he would move to another country if he could afford to do so.

"You play in a cocoon in Uganda," Wanyama says. "There is so little contact with the outside world in chess that it is hard to improve relative to the better players elsewhere, because you don't get the competition outside of the Olympiad. There is a ceiling here and if you grow tall enough in the game you just keep banging your head."

All four of Phiona's female Olympiad teammates acknowledge serious doubts about their futures in chess. Joan Butindo married Stephen Kawuma in 2011, moved to England, and says she'd like to compete in future Olympiads, but it will depend largely on her husband's level of interest in the game. Ivy, Grace, and Rita all graduated in the same class from Kampala's Makerere University in 2011 and now must support themselves financially.

"There are many hurdles," Ivy says. "Time is a problem. Money. Attitude is a very big issue. You look into the future and you ask yourself, 'Why am I suffering for chess?' The only motivation that makes us come to most tournaments is hoping we can win some money, but then if we lose on the first day, sometimes we don't show up on the second day. We are the biggest obstacles to ourselves. You have to have an overly positive attitude and once that falters, you're finished. It's a hard world."

Like many women in Uganda, Ivy has not always been encouraged to pursue sports, even by members of her own family.

"When I started shining in chess my dad could not accept that," Ivy says. "I told him I was going to Russia to play in the Chess Olympiad and he said, 'Yeah, you can do chess, but I want you to excel more in your studies.' It's very disheartening. Just once say you're proud of me without bringing in the 'but.' Every time I dream about chess, he has to say 'but.' I could be so much better with some support."

Some talented female players in Uganda have given up chess after getting married because their husbands forbid them to play. It is also telling that none of Phiona's teammates on the national team are older than their mid-20s because that is the age when most women in Uganda can no longer concentrate as intently on the sport.

Grace is diverted from the game by an interest in music and the need to find a job. "I have gone to school and studied accounting, but that's not my passion," Grace says. "I must do it to earn a living. The most common thing that takes a Ugandan chess player away from the game is work. I am one of a number of women in Uganda who would love to focus on chess alone and take it on as a career, but in our country chess cannot put food on the table."

Ivy plans to become a lawyer because she also sees no future in chess.

"I won't base my career on chess because realistically in Uganda what can you become? A chess coach? A chess teacher? Maybe as a side job. You get a few students. But career-wise, no. Uganda won't allow it."

Like Grace, Rita also has a degree in accounting and talks dreamily about how she will earn money as an accountant and use it to form a club to teach young girls the game of chess. She, too, wants to go to more Olympiads, if time permits, but she recognizes the difference between her situation and that of Phiona. "Phiona grew up on the streets and she stays in the slum and that's why I try to treat her like my own sister," Rita says. "I absolutely pray that Phiona continues to play chess, because I think chess is a light for her. It's like a torch that can take her out of the slum to people who may be able to look after her. I always tell Phiona not to ever leave chess."

There has never been a titled female chess player in Ugandan history. When it comes to their futures in chess, the big ladies don't dream of titles or ratings, just more trips out of Uganda. Only Phiona has aspirations to be great in the game. All of Phiona's Olympiad teammates agree that Phiona is blessed by her youth to continue to pursue the game and that her potential is immense, but that her biggest hurdle is herself.

"It's tricky to figure her out because one day Phiona will play and you won't be that impressed and the next day she'll play and you'll think, 'Oh my God this girl is so incredibly talented,'" Grace says. "She lacks consistency and that's probably because her background is so inconsistent."

Says Rita, "When I look at Phiona she just needs attention. She needs love. She needs people who care about her and encourage her. I look at her and I think that once I get a big job in a few years, I will sponsor Phiona in each and every tournament in the world."

"Phiona is a very good player, but she could be even better if she really believed in herself," Ivy says. "It's hard for someone to step out of the slum thinking that the world is at my feet and I'm going to conquer it. That takes a big, big, big heart to have such an attitude. We all know how good Phiona is. Sometimes I think we know it more than she does."

The magazine covers stuck up on the walls inside shacks around Katwe are usually there to cover a hole, but the faces pictured on them are significant. Beyonce. Serena Williams. Michelle Obama. For the most part, the girls of Katwe need to be told who these people are and once they learn, they want to be just like them. For Phiona Mutesi and the other teenage girls of Katwe, there are no true female role models to follow. Nothing realistic. Nothing attainable. No solid businesswoman or stable homemaker. There is no in-between for Phiona to grab onto during a very impressionable time in her life, a time when she needs a lot of guidance about becoming an adult.

"Phiona is beginning to blossom into a woman, but she wears loose clothes and covers herself up because it's such a hard thing in the slum to be single and be a young woman," Rodney Suddith says. "It would help if Phiona could find a female role model to help her figure out who she is."

Instead, Phiona seems guided by a man. More of a phantom, really.

Phiona has been told by those who knew him that she is her father's daughter, strong and resilient and fierce when challenged. But she never knew her father. She has no memories of him. She doesn't even know what he looked like. The only photograph Harriet once had of Godfrey Buyinza was lost long ago in a Katwe flood.

"There are times when I feel I miss my father," Phiona says. "For example my mother has not bought me any clothes since I was nine years old. If my father was there, I think he would have bought me clothes since I was nine. I love my mother and I sympathize with her. She struggles to look for food and pay for rent, so how can I ask her for money for clothes? But I believe my father would have met all that."

Harriet never talks about her late husband. It is only when one of her children asks her for something that she cannot afford, that she says, "Did your father leave me with any money?"

Phiona has learned not to ask her mother about her father and she discourages any talk about him from her older siblings.

"I don't really know anything concerning my father and I don't want to know," Phiona says. "Sometimes my older brother and sister will try to tell me things concerning our dad and they could tell me the kind of life that was there before he died. I really even end up sad and tell myself I wish he was still alive. If he was still alive then we wouldn't be suffering the way we are suffering. So that's why I don't want anyone to talk about him."

Part of Buyinza's legacy for his daughter is a threat of AIDS. Phiona learned several years ago that her father died of AIDS, which makes her wonder if she might also have the virus. There are 1.2 million people in Uganda infected with HIV and more than 100,000 Ugandans die of AIDS every year. For years Harriet refused to be tested because she feared the stigma that a positive result carries in Uganda, shunning from her community and possibly even her own family. But Harriet says that in recent years she has been tested three times and has always tested negative for the HIV virus. Harriet has never spoken to Phiona about HIV and while the subject is discussed in school, Phiona is still relatively naive to the causes of the disease.

"I know a bit about AIDS," Phiona says. "I know this kind of disease you can get through adultery or sharing piercing instruments. When you love a man and you don't go for a blood test you can give birth to children who can end up also becoming victims."

While Phiona is well aware of the possibility that she has the virus, she has not been tested because children in Uganda are rarely tested before the age of 18. Katende may encourage her to be tested sooner so that she might begin treatment with the necessary medicine if she is found to be positive.

Phiona has known dozens of people in Katwe who have died of AIDS. She is surrounded by tragedy daily. Inside the chess project alone she has observed as a fellow player, Alawi Katwere, became ill with a mysterious disease that first discolored his skin and then stopped his heart. She knows another girl from the project who was gang-raped and then abandoned by her family because her medical treatment cost too much money. She knows another girl from the project who twice aborted her own children with a coat hanger and nearly died of the trauma.

"These kids in Katwe are at the bottom and many Ugandans want them to stay at the bottom," Suddith says. "It's a form of prejudice. People in the slums are recognized as human, but that's about it. For anyone in Katwe to achieve anything is a big thing. So as much as we're excited about Phiona's accomplishments, there's a deep concern over how she'll handle all of this. The fact that she's a teenager now, many believe she should already be a mother. Warding off guys who just want to sleep with her is part of her daily routine. Phiona's life is so fragile. Katwe is a fallen world. It is a war zone and you can only dodge bullets for so long."

As long as Phiona is in the slum, she must keep dodging those bullets. Clearing those hurdles. She's a girl who must avoid becoming the woman who every single day Katwe keeps pushing her to be. She must keep struggling to heed the cautionary tale she has witnessed so clearly and painfully in her own sister.

Night's daughter Rita was kidnapped sometime toward the beginning of 2011, though it seems so much longer ago than that to her mother. Night isn't exactly sure how long her daughter has been gone. She knows only that Rita was four years old when she was abducted and that she is older now. And still gone.

Days before Rita was abducted, Night ran into a man that she once knew when she lived in the Nateete slum. The man greeted her and asked, "Where do you stay?" Then one afternoon, when Night was away working with her mother at the Kibuye market and had left her children at home, that man came to her shack. He brought a gift of popcorn for her children. Then he took Rita.

"When I arrived home, one of my older daughters, Winnie, showed me the way the man had left with Rita and I tried to follow him up," Night says. "When I reached where he used to stay, they told me that they knew the man but he had already been chased away from the village. When I reached the police they told me that they too knew the man and they had many cases against him."

Unable to find the man, Night sought out his wife. With some support from other members of the wife's village, Night was able to lead her to the police station and the woman admitted that her husband had taken Rita, but that they had gone to Kasese district, which is more than 300 kilometers from Kampala.

"So when the policemen heard the woman confess that my daughter is there, they told the woman to take me to where Rita is staying," Night says. "But this woman suggested that unless I had 200,000 shillings for transport that I won't be in position to go there. So I tried my best to look for the money and I failed to get it. I think about Rita all the time, but what can I do? I cannot afford to go try to find her. So I look after the other three children as best I can."

Rita is the third oldest of the four children Night has conceived with two different men, along with Eva, 10, Winnie, 7, and two-year-old Grace. Night has stayed with each of the men in the hope of supporting her children and sometimes her mother and siblings. Night also works at the market, where Harriet has subcontracted her business so that Night can sell curry powder and tea leaves while her mother sells vegetables. Night's other job is with a local tailor who makes children's clothes. The tailor prices a dress at 1,000 shillings and if Night is able to hawk it on the street for 1,500 shillings, she keeps the difference.

Night is now about 27 years old. She has walked a very similar path as her mother, often sacrificing herself to try to save the rest of her family. Phiona is at the crossroads age when Night's life turned for the worse, when Night committed herself to help get her family off the street at the risk of her own future. Harriet's two surviving daughters maintain a complicated relationship.

"I remember there were times when we were younger and I would tell Night, 'Stop giving birth to children,' because when she gave birth their fathers often denied them, so we had nothing to do apart from still allowing them to stay with us," Phiona says. "I realized that the food we were using for four people couldn't be enough for us and for Night and her children, but she continued to have more children."

Night believes that Phiona doesn't understand her situation, doesn't grasp the sacrifices she has made, and worries that her younger sister doesn't respect her.

"I try to advise her, but personally I believe Phiona despises me in a way because she sees me as though I'm really low in status to her," Night says. "I rarely see her because I stay in a different place, but if I somehow find her home, I'll tell her, 'Phiona, the opportunity you have, make good use of it, because I did not have such an opportunity. Make sure you study hard, because you can see the kind of life I have now. I don't have any chance and I will never be happy as you are.' Whenever I advise her, she says to me she has understood what I have told her, but I don't know whether she leaves everything there. I don't know."

Night is on the wrong side of the dividing line, born too early to potentially have been rescued by Robert Katende's chess project. Now she must be saved by her sister, just as she saved Phiona from the streets many years ago in a very different way.

"I remember one day one of my daughters was sick and I didn't have any money on me and Phiona gave me money she won playing chess and I was able to take that kid to the hospital," Night says. "Whenever Phiona gets money, she buys items for my children and promises me that if it is possible she will make sure that they go to school. For sure, when I'm having serious problems and she has some money she does not hesitate to extend support to me."

When Night is asked about her dreams for the future, a sadness envelops her. "The way I see it, I don't have any hope," Night says. "I have no dreams. All I need is to see my children studying. And maybe have someplace to live where they can find me."

When Night is asked about her dreams for Phiona, she simply says, "That she would not lead my life."

Chapter 11
Dreams

Phiona Mutesi in front of the Agape Church where she
trains to realize her dream of becoming a Grandmaster.

Agape Church could collapse at any moment. It is a ramshackle structure that lists alarmingly to one side, barely held together by scrap wood, rope, a few nails, and faith. It is disposable, like everything else around it.

Inside Agape on this Saturday morning are 37 children whose lives are equally rickety. They dribble in from all over Katwe to play a game that none of them had ever heard of before they met Robert Katende. When the children walk through the door, grins crease their hardened faces. This is home as much as any place in their lives. It is a refuge, the only community they know. These are their friends, their brothers and sisters of chess, if not of blood, and there is relative safety and comfort here. It is a place to be that they can count on, a place that is predictable, a place where the competition is not to survive but simply to win a game. Inside Agape it is almost possible to forget the chaos outside the doorway.

Now in its eighth year, Katende's chess project relocated to Agape at the beginning of 2010 from its roots at Bishop John Michael Mugerwa's veranda. There are only seven chessboards inside and chess pieces are so scarce that sometimes an orphan pawn must stand in for a king. A child sits on each end of a wobbly bench, which acts as a pew for Sunday services, both straddling the board between their knobby knees with captured pieces guarded in their laps. Those who aren't playing gather around the boards to study players they admire. A five-year-old kid in a threadbare Denver Broncos jersey with #7 on the back competes against an 11-year-old in a T-shirt that reads J'ADORE PARIS. One of the game's spectators wears a discolored shirt that reads S.O.I. CHESS ACADEMY. Most of the kids are barefoot. Some wear flip-flops. One has on black wingtips with no laces.

It is rapid-fire street chess. When more than a few seconds elapse without a move, there is a palpable restlessness. It is remarkably quiet except for the violent thud of one piece slaying another and the occasional dispute over location of a piece on a board so faded that the dark squares are barely distinguishable from the light. Surrender is signaled by a clattering of the opponent's captured pieces onto the board. There is rarely any celebration from the victor, more often a humble piece of advice to the vanquished on how best to avoid the trap that decided the game, always the more experienced players teaching the others what they know. It is an individual sport being played by kids who have been forged by their harsh environment to look out only for themselves, yet these children are a team. The Children's Team. Each one of them contributing to a greater whole.

Phiona Mutesi arrives without ceremony and takes her place in the audience of her brother Brian's game. The girl who was initially spurned by the other children for being too dirty has become a sort of den mother for the chess project. Phiona is a patient teacher who, whenever she's asked, will share remarkable stories of her travels. The younger children in the project sit close to her, watching and listening intently. They often ask why she has made a specific move. Phiona explains it to them and tells them that if they work hard they can someday exceed her in the game.

Katende wanders from board to board, sometimes sitting to play, sometimes suggesting moves, always searching for a teaching point, whether it be in chess or in life. There is no timetable at the project. After several hours of chess, a few of the kids volunteer to cook the porridge in three rusty saucepans. When it is ready and poured into bowls, the children who are not involved in a game line up to eat, while those playing don't leave their boards until their games are over. Because there are no spoons, everybody eats with their hands. Many of the kids consume their porridge ravenously because they have not eaten anything since this same bowl of porridge the previous day.

Katende sits among a small group of children who are licking porridge from their fingers. He agrees to tell them their favorite story, the one about St. Peter from the Bible. The other kids gradually gather around, one by one, from all corners of the church, until all of them are huddled around Katende, even though most have heard this tale before. When Katende speaks, his words take on the power of a sermon:

"One time when Jesus was with his disciples, one of his disciples called St. Peter walked on water. St. Peter was with all of his other friends on the boat and he saw Jesus coming on the water walking and someone asked, 'Master, are you telling me to come?' The rest feared. But St. Peter was the one who stepped out of the boat. It wasn't an easy situation. It is extraordinary. Unrealistic. How do you get out of the boat then step on the water when you know you are definitely going to drown? But that's when you realize it was a miracle. He could do it. If he hadn't stepped out, there would be no miracle. So that's why sometimes we need to get out of our boats to realize a miracle. We can't just sit back and wait for a miracle to happen.

"We don't have. But if we don't have what we desire to have, then we realize we have to think, 'What can we do with the little we have?' Because no one is here without anything. But the issue is, how can I work with the little I have to go to another level? Because many times people spend a lot of time thinking about what they don't have and this has also changed my life. If you ask me how was I able to keep sponsoring myself for school, I can't tell you because I don't know. A miracle happened. But it was after I took a step and then a miracle occurred. I got a loan and I started studying and I played soccer for the school and after the first semester that's when the dean said this guy is playing very well and we can give him some money for schooling. It didn't find me. I had to take the bold step. Then after the second semester, they said that this guy is a good player, other schools will give him a full scholarship, we must do that or they will take him. My aim was not to go there to play soccer, it was to achieve my academics. All these miracles started happening, but only after I took the first step. If I had not taken the first step, I would have been nowhere.

"We shouldn't have excuses. Personally my life is a testimony and I've shared my life story with all of you. Some of you think you are suffering but you have not yet gone through what I went through. But I'm here. You all say, 'Coach is well off,' but I'm not yet where I want to be, but at least where I am is not where I would have been if I had not really worked hard. It depends on you, but there is always a way out, but how do we make it happen?

"So St. Peter stepped out of the boat and he went to where Jesus was. For all of you, learning chess has not been a walkover. For all of you it involved diligence, commitment, determination, faith, and then being here day after day. But through that because you turned up for the program, someone came in and said, 'Hey, these kids are doing well in chess, but they are not studying. If they can do well in chess, then given an opportunity to study they can do well in school.' This education has not come because someone found you out there. It is because you took a step to come for the program. Other people dropped off, but you kept on coming.

"If you show that kind of character, you need no excuses. Even when there is tragedy you know life must continue still. You just recorrect yourself and say, 'What next? I need to go on. Life needs to continue. I don't have this, I don't have this, I don't have this, but what do I have?' You cannot even complete the list of what you don't have. It is huge. Now forget that. Don't even think about what you don't have. Ask yourself, 'What do I have?' After having that list of what you have, then assess yourself and ask, 'What are my abilities? What can I do to live? Where can I apply this?' Then you use what you do have to get what you don't have on the list. Each one of you is realizing a miracle because you had the courage to step out of the boat. All of you can walk on water."

218

Benjamin and Ivan sat on either end of a bench one day at Agape, a chessboard in between them, when Benjamin first told Ivan about his dream to be a Grandmaster.

The more cautious of the two, Ivan said, "You know, Benja, those Grandmasters, they spend a lot of time on training. They have all the facilities. For us we have to struggle for what we eat, so it will be so hard for us to make it there."

"We have been to Sudan and become champions when we didn't think that was possible," Benjamin said. "Why can't we also be Grandmasters?"

Rather than dwell on who they are, the children of the chess project like to talk about who they want to be. They dream. The biggest difference between the children inside Agape Church and those outside is the capacity to dream.

Benjamin, who like most of the children in the chess project attends school on a Popp Scholarship, dreams of becoming a doctor. Ivan dreams of becoming a telecommunications engineer. Joseph Asaba dreams of becoming a bank manager. Richard Tugume dreams of becoming an electrical engineer. Gloria Nansubuga dreams of becoming a GM. When Gloria, who is about 11 years old, is asked what a GM is, she admits that she doesn't really know. She just knows that is the goal that everyone else in the chess project aspires to, but not what the letters actually stand for. It doesn't matter to her. Gloria wants to be a GM, and considering her blossoming talent, her age, and her accomplished tutor, she may have the best chance of them all. "That Phiona has been able to go to other countries and she has won, that is my inspiration," Gloria says. "She is not only very masterful in the game, but she is very kind. Phiona is now my role model. I was first her teacher, but she is now the one teaching me. Phiona believes I can become a GM."

Ever since Phiona's brother Brian was seriously injured in the bicycle accident, he has dreamed of becoming a doctor. "I realize that if I become a doctor then from that I can open up a hospital someday. If anyone in my family ever had to be fixed, I would not have to worry about paying for it. I believe the chess program in the slum will still be running by then and I want to be in position to support the children who will be in that program. When they are coming to the hospital, I will be treating them for free."

Phiona's 13-year-old brother, Richard, who joined the Katwe chess project shortly after his sister, attends primary school and often sleeps in the project's storage shed to be closer to school. He dreams of becoming an electrical engineer.

"When I grow up I want to be many things," says Samuel Mayanja, one of the Pioneers. "First, I want to be a medical doctor. I want to be a Grandmaster. I want be an engineer and I want also to be a movie producer."

Overhearing this list, Katende smiled and asked, "Mayanja, have you ever heard of any one person succeeding in all of those fields?

Samuel's resolve was unshaken. "Why not?" Samuel says. "Why can I not be the first?"

Inspired by the success of Phiona and Benjamin and Ivan, they all want to stick with chess, to join the national team, to travel to future Olympiads. The slum kids, who were initially rejected by the country's chess establishment, now are considered the backbone of Uganda's promising future in the game.

"In the years to come I believe Coach Robert's kids will fill our national team," Godfrey Gali says. "The wealthier kids in the school system cannot win games against them. They complain to me that they don't receive the same training. In future Olympiads, I believe our teams will be made up entirely of kids from the slums. They are driven by the kind of life they lead. There is a desperation in the way they play that you don't see in the other kids. You play harder when the outcome may decide if you eat that night."

Most of Katende's chess children also aspire to someday teach the game, to follow in their mentor's footsteps. They hope to mirror and honor the man who has helped save them by saving others like them in the slums.

"I want to train many, many children to play chess because I remember when Coach told me to train Benjamin and now I see Benjamin is a very good player and a very good person," Ivan says. "That motivates me and I feel I can also train other players to be successful, just as Coach Robert does."

Katende has dreams as well. Based on the model he has established with Phiona and the children she tutors at Naalya Estates, Katende aspires to open a chess academy where the children of the project can teach the children of more affluent families how to play the game. It is part of his ultimate dream to open a Children's Home that will provide a place to live for disenfranchised kids, orphans, and abused children, including children from the chess project.

After passing on potential opportunities several years ago to play soccer professionally in Argentina, Denmark, and Vietnam because he could not afford to travel to those places to try out for interested clubs, Katende says he no longer dreams of soccer. He no longer dreams of playing on that lush green field. He plays only on the Good News Football Club, where his greatest fulfillment occurs after the games.

He has dedicated his life to backing up a vow he made one day as a student in S2 during his five-kilometer walk home from school, when he turned to a friend and said, "We have to make sure we study hard so that our children won't have to walk the way we have walked. My children will not suffer the way I have."

In 2008 Katende handed over the soccer portion of his project to other Sports Outreach ministers so he could concentrate all of his efforts on the chess program, which he continues to expand to more slum areas in Kampala. With the help of Aloysius Kyazze, Katende has even brought the program to Sports Outreach's other headquarters in Gulu, in the northern part of Uganda, where 40 children competed in their first chess tournament in 2010. That tournament was run by Gerald Mutyaba, a former Pioneer, who acts as Gulu's version of Coach Robert.

The 30-year-old Katende sees himself as an example of what a little hope and help and some exposure to a more stable life can produce.

"I have experienced many lives," Katende says. "I was in a poor state and when I left my grandma I came to a moderately better place where my mother and I were renting in the slums. Then when she died I moved to my auntie's place, which was a better place again, and with her I saw many new things and I asked myself, 'That means people can live like this?' With my grandma, when it rained I got a banana leaf to cover myself, but Aunt Jacent had a vehicle and when it rained they could just drive to school. I wanted to do whatever I could to make sure that I could be like those people who live a better life. That's where my drive comes from and I want these children to follow my lead."

To that end, Katende has invited Phiona and the other chess children to landmark events in his life, so that they can see for themselves what living a more normal life looks like. "I took four of the chess children to my introduction to my wife's family," Katende says. "I wanted them to see that. It is easy to tell them, 'You must wait until time comes when you find the right person to marry and then you get introduced properly to the family.' But that's mere talking. They can ask, 'Coach, have you done that?' It is now more clear to them. They've witnessed it and now they tell me they want to do that as well."

About 20 children from his Katwe project attended Katende's wedding in June of 2010 to Sarah Ntongo, whom he'd met three years earlier when she volunteered as a teacher at the Kampala School for the Physically Handicapped, which shares its compound with Sports Outreach Institute. During school holidays, Katende has also invited many of the children to stay with him and his wife at the modest two-room house they rent in the Mengo-Lungujja district, less than three kilometers from Katwe.

Katende also tries to provide some financial support to his extended family whenever possible.

"Robert is my Lord," says Katende's grandmother, Aidah Namusisi, who believes she is 93 years old and still lives in the Kasubi slum with other relatives. "He is the one who takes care of me. He's the one who looks after all of us. Whatever good things we are to get, he is the one who can get it for us."

Katende has become the role model for his entire family. The same framed photograph of Katende dressed in cap and gown graduating from university is prominently displayed in the sitting rooms of both Aunt Jacent and Aunt Dez.

"I believe Robert's mother looks down on him from above and she is very, very happy to see the way he is right now," Aunt Dez says. "She died lamenting and crying because of her son, but you cannot really refuse God's plan. Right before she died, Robert's mother told me, 'That son of mine. I don't want him to become a hooligan. I don't want him to become a thief. I want him to become a son who our country is proud of.' Knowing what he's done for these children, I believe her last wish has been granted."

Katende's first child arrived in dramatic fashion when his wife was taken to the hospital delivery room, but the baby would not come. Doctors allotted Sarah a half hour, after which they said they would need to perform a Caesarean section. Katende anguished over that possibility because he did not have enough money to pay for the expensive procedure. Thirty minutes elapsed without change, but doctors were delayed for another half hour. Just as they arrived to take Sarah to the operating room, she went into labor and had a normal birth, sparing her family the anguish and expense of an operation that they could not afford. Katende's daughter was born on April 26, 2011.

He named her Mercy.

In Uganda it is said, "Giving birth to a daughter is like giving birth to sugar." Female children are viewed by many Ugandans as assets. Dowry. When it comes time for marriage, they are worth a negotiable number of cattle, which explains why many Ugandan men see women as property. Some fathers have even been known to forbid daughters from marrying until they find a husband wealthy enough to pay a dowry that can help the rest of the bride's family survive.

Women in Uganda don't often get to dream for themselves. It's a male-dominated society, so everything Phiona has accomplished has come with the assistance of men.

When Bishop Mugerwa was approached by Robert Katende years ago and asked about the use of his veranda to shelter his chess program, Mugerwa had never heard of chess.

"I never expected chess to catch on," Mugerwa says. "I thought it was promoting laziness because I saw the kids just sat there for hours and hours. I am shocked at what has happened. By using chess to travel out of Katwe, Phiona is carrying a message to the other kids that slum children are not a waste, not forgotten, not a lost generation. These kids just lack leadership because there is usually no one successful to imitate. Phiona is their role model. We are a neighborhood full of children who think they are nobodies and she is making kids believe they can be somebody. Phiona is my hero and I believe she can be all of Uganda's hero."

Katende chuckles about how some of the same mothers in Harriet's neighborhood who feared the mzungu and forbade their children from joining the chess program at its inception, sheepishly approached Harriet a few years later asking how their children could attend. He acknowledges that he never expected this level of success or exposure. It was never his goal. He was just looking for a forum to relate to the children at his project who didn't play soccer. Now he has created a pipeline for them to potentially escape the slum.

"Frankly, I never imagined Phiona making the national team," Katende says. "My purpose was not for Phiona to be great at chess, but to have a way that I could share my faith with her, make her a good citizen, and see her life transformed through fear of the Lord. Now I see that maybe she can be more."

Because she had dropped out of school completely for two years along with parts of four others before the Popp Scholarship opportunity arose in 2006, Phiona has only reached S2 at St. Mbuga Secondary School and has four years remaining there. Phiona is in the top 20 percent of her class academically and Katende believes that if she continues to concentrate on her studies she has a chance to earn a government scholarship to university just as he once did.

"I want Phiona to understand that her way out of the slum is a combination of studying very hard and pursuing chess greatly," Katende says. "Ask most kids when they finish secondary school what they want to become and they don't know. Ugandan kids are not trained to do jobs. There is no path. Studying alone is not a sure deal. You need to have contacts. In Uganda it is more about *know who* than know how. Nobody is certain how they will survive, but Phiona's chess can possibly produce a contact. It is the only advantage she has."

"The goal is that chess will help her find a way out of that slum and she will have an improved life and when that is witnessed by other kids it will be profound," Rodney Suddith says. "If Phiona can escape, the others will follow. Then if they can find their way out, they are going to want the same for their brothers and sisters and cousins and eventually their kids. This chess program could be an ongoing means for kids to not only grow in the game, but a means to an education, a means to a job, which is a means to a healthy family. With this chess program of forty kids in it, you think, 'What if twenty of these kids went to university because of this? That means that there are twenty parents who went to school who now have kids that are living a better life.'"

While Katende says he hopes through her chess that Phiona can begin to blaze a trail out of the slum for his other chess kids to follow, he remains realistic. He knows that for her to accomplish that, Phiona likely must produce success in chess on a world stage like no other Ugandan, man or woman, has ever achieved.

"That path has a lot of struggles," Katende admits. "Unless an opportunity comes up where she has a chance to train at a higher level, she may put in a lot but it may not match the standard out there in the rest of the world. If she gets funds, I believe she can go to another level. That is just a dream. Sometimes you don't even want to talk about it because it seems impossible. But we have to move by faith. If we've already been able to achieve things that we never expected, then we don't lose the hope. Surely, we cannot know the end because there are so many questions left to answer."

Can she keep improving in chess without a more advanced coach?
Can she improve without books or a computer?
Can she improve without sponsorship?
Can she really become a Grandmaster?
Can the attention to her story make her a target in Katwe?
Can she avoid the pressure to become a mother?
Can she still thrive if she has HIV?
Can she get out of Katwe?
Can she stay out?

The true magic of Phiona's journey lies in the remarkable breadth of possibilities. Even if Phiona can somehow produce the means to leave Katwe, then history has proven that her struggle is just beginning. Nearly all of the stories of people leaving Katwe end with their return. Can Phiona really break the chain?

"She's got this pull in two directions and that's a dilemma for her," Suddith says. "For Phiona to succeed, realistically she has to separate from the slums and that's going to be harder than people think. She's so sensitive and she is going to have a very hard time moving away from her family, who may pressure her to stay. I've learned that you can't pull someone out of Katwe. You have to walk out with them side by side. Phiona could walk out with Robert, but she can't pull her sister out. She can't pull her mother out. If they are not willing to walk, they may pull her back."

Both Suddith and Katende express concern that Phiona is a role model without a role model. They understand that the further Phiona strides from the life she's known, the more they may have to fill that void.

"Phiona's eyes have really opened to the idea that she has a gift and she's become very curious about how to handle that," Suddith says. "She asks me questions like 'What would I do if I worked in the big city?' or 'How do you go shopping?' It's fascinating. She's seeking information. For the first time she is starting to ask questions about life that her mother cannot answer. Harriet is not a life teacher. She's lived a very hard life and she knows she doesn't want the same life for her daughter, but her experiential reality is that she can't really help her."

Harriet is just another denizen of Katwe who once dreamed of getting out, but tragic circumstances prevented her from leading a better life than those before her. She arrived in Katwe as a young child and has never left and she doesn't see beyond "just there." Harriet simply aspires to be a religious servant and hopes her daughter will do the same.

"I want Phiona to be a child that is pleasing to God," Harriet says. "I am also very sure that if she continues with chess she will meet good people and live a good life."

When Harriet is asked if she believes that her daughter will leave Katwe, she pauses for a moment and then says, "I have never thought about that."

Phiona Mutesi is the ultimate underdog. To be African is to be an underdog in the world. To be Ugandan is to be an underdog in Africa. To be from Katwe is to be an underdog in Uganda. To be a girl is to be an underdog in Katwe.

When asked about her dreams, Phiona ponders the question for a long time, as if it is necessary to inventory them all in her mind. "Okay, what I think is to study hard and perform well in chess in order to be able to get the money to lift up my family," Phiona says. "That is where my dreams begin."

Phiona says that she dreams to someday be married to a man of her choosing, married in the true sense of the word, unlike her mother and her sister who have referred to themselves as "married" but were never officially wed. Phiona dreams of having children, but not for many years and not, she has vowed to her family, until she and her husband are secure enough financially to support those children. "I expect that to happen many years ahead," Phiona says. "I dream to have two children, a boy and a girl, but only after I have planned for them, not like the way we are at home when you give birth to many children you can't take care of. Me, I expect to take the best care of my children."

Phiona dreams to someday be a Grandmaster, but considering the hurdles involved, Katende has impressed upon her the need for a backup plan.

Phiona dreams to someday be a nurse. When Harriet learns of this, she smiles proudly and places both hands over her heart. "Phiona never told me that," Harriet says. "One time when we were in the house we were talking and I said to her that I had once dreamed of being a nurse because those people looked so nice to me and the way they conduct themselves fills my heart with joy. My dream was not able to be fulfilled, but God has again revealed it through my daughter."

Phiona's favorite place to dream is at home late at night with her brothers, Brian and Richard, lying down beside her. Their fondest shared dream is about building a house. A place that doesn't flood. A place where they will no longer fear an angry landlord's knock on the door. A place they own.

"There is one dream I have beyond all others," Phiona says. "I imagine living in a home where all the suffering, all the challenges we have been through would be over."

During their many discussions, the three siblings have devised a mental blueprint for their house. It will have eight rooms with windows made of glass, including a dining room with flowers on the table and a sitting room with a comfortable sofa and chairs, and everyone will have their own bedroom with their own bed. The house will not have stairs because it is assumed that by that time Harriet will be too old to climb them. The plans also include a large compound filled with trees where Night's children can play, surrounded by a secure gate and fencing and tiles in the ground between the gate and the front door so that visitors will not have to step in mud to reach the house. There will be fans on the ceilings to regulate the air and there will be toilets to sit on that flush with water. And a television that plays DVDs. And a water tap inside the house. And some electric lamps. And a fridge. There is a continuing disagreement among the siblings over whether a swimming pool will be affordable.

"Our dream is about our whole family living a better life there, a life that we deserve to be in," Brian says. "So we want someplace where we could really feel so secure when we are staying there."

All that is left undecided is where the building will stand.

"We are not bothered about the location," Phiona says. "As long as it is anywhere else apart from the slums and it belongs to us."

When the sermon is over, the porridge dishes cleaned and stored away, an early evening rainstorm beating on the tin roof of the Agape Church and beginning to flood Katwe, they come back to chess.

Katende is still there, much later than he'd planned to be as usual, along with Ivan and Benjamin and Samuel and Richard and Brian and tiny Gloria, and up beside the pulpit there is 16-year-old Phiona Mutesi, one of the best chess players in the world, juggling three games at once and dominating them all. Phiona stalks her young opponents as ruthlessly yet compassionately as she can, while drawing a flower in the dirt on the floor with her toe, plotting her next move.

Acknowledgments

One of the first questions I'm asked whenever I speak to anyone about the story of Phiona Mutesi is, "How did you ever hear about her?"

The gentleman who shared Phiona's story with me, Troy Buder, learned of it by reading an article written by Rodney Suddith in a Sports Outreach newsletter. Buder skimmed through the story about three slum children winning a chess tournament in Sudan and then threw out the newsletter. Later that day, Buder retrieved it out of his office trash can, because he couldn't get the story out of his mind. Buder tells me that scenario occurred several more times until one day in March of 2010 when he attended an event where I was speaking. Buder approached me afterward to share Phiona's extraordinary story, and I can't thank him enough for doing so.

I promptly wrote a proposal and sent it to ESPN, where it wound up in the hands of brilliant *ESPN The Magazine* editor J. B. Morris, who assigned me to travel to Uganda to meet Phiona in September of 2010. Within hours of my arrival at Agape Church in Katwe, I realized that Phiona's story was much bigger than just a magazine article. I knew I needed to write this book.

The logistics of conducting interviews in a Ugandan slum are daunting, and frankly, *The Queen of Katwe* would not exist without the herculean efforts of Robert Katende. Not only did Katende spend countless hours sharing his personal story with me, but he also arranged and acted as my translator for almost every interview featured in this book. Since my most recent trip to Kampala in August of 2011, I have spoken with Katende regularly, asking for his help with everything from tournament results and historical research to coordinating a photo shoot. Thank you so much, Robert.

I also offer my heartfelt thanks to Harriet Nakku, her children, and all of the other Ugandans I had the pleasure to meet and talk to for this project. While their names are too numerous to include here, their courage is inspirational, and without them I would not have been able to tell this story. I also want to thank Patrick Wolff, an American chess Grandmaster who generously shared his expertise, and especially Russ Carr, Rodney Suddith, and Norm and Tricia Popp for their participation in this book, but more importantly, for everything they have done, and continue to do, to help the people of Uganda.

I am also deeply thankful to my editor at Scribner, Paul Whitlatch, for his exceptional instincts in helping me chisel this story from a boulder, as well as his Simon & Schuster colleagues Nan Graham, Susan Moldow, Roz Lippel, Lauren Lavelle, Brian Belfiglio, and Rex Bonomelli. I also owe an enormous debt of gratitude to my agent, Chris Parris-Lamb, whose initial unbridled excitement about the story of a Ugandan chess player encouraged me to pursue it.

Of course, thank you to my amazing wife, Dana, my awesome kids, Atticus and Sawyer, and the rest of my family for enduring two years of near-total preoccupation, when my mind was often in Katwe even if my body was at home.

During my most recent trip to Uganda, I will never forget sitting on the porch of the Pope Paul Memorial Hotel in Kampala each night with Rodney Suddith reveling in the remarkable story unfolding before me. At the end of each evening, we shared our favorite moment, what Suddith called the "snapshot of the day," and I am so grateful to him for always finding a blessing where I had merely seen an interview.

Acknowledgments

Finally, my most essential thanks must go to Phiona Mutesi for trusting me to share her remarkable story in this book that someday soon, as her English continues to improve, I expect she will be able to read herself. I am eager to discover what happens next.

New Postscript for
the Paperback Edition

Sometime, probably in 2006, Phiona Mutesi sat on the floor of a dusty veranda in the Katwe slum playing chess when she was approached by a boy who wanted to show her a book. Ten-year-old Phiona had never seen a book about chess. Phiona couldn't read well, so she flipped through the pages until a photograph caught her eye. Phiona asked the boy, "Who is this guy?" The boy described the man in the photo, Garry Kasparov, as a world champion and a Grandmaster. Phiona had never heard of a "Grandmaster" before. When Phiona's coach, Robert Katende, explained the title to her, at that moment Phiona decided that a Grandmaster is everything she wanted to be. Kasparov became her idol.

Readers may notice that *The Queen of Katwe* doesn't really end. It pauses. Since this book was first published, Phiona's story continues to develop. It has been fascinating to watch her progress.

During our final interviews for the book in early 2012, Phiona and Katende had begun focusing on that summer's Chess Olympiad in Istanbul, Turkey. During preparations to qualify for that event, Katende suggested that Phiona compete in the boys division of Uganda's annual national schools tournament in April, which had a more accomplished slate of players.

"I realized that Phiona competing against the girls in that tournament would not give her a good platform for training," Katende says. "So I decided that although it has never happened in the history of Uganda, I would field her in for the boys team."

Says Phiona, "When Coach told me I would play for the boys team, I became nervous because I had never done it before. But when I started playing the first game, I put out my best play and when I won that game, I started realizing that I think I could make it all the way through."

Phiona played on Board 1 representing the St. Mbuga Secondary School boys team alongside teammates Benjamin Mukumbya, Richard Tugume, and her brother Brian Mugabi, all of whom learned the game in Katende's chess program in Katwe. Phiona played a total of 11 games in the tournament against boys from schools all over Uganda. She lost only one game, earning a gold medal as she helped St. Mbuga win its fourth consecutive schools tournament title.

In June, Phiona began the qualifying tournament for the 2012 Olympiad.

"The competition was very stiff and I knew that if I was to lose any game I would definitely be off the team," Phiona says. "The most challenging game of all was against Ivy. I was having a very bad position on the board and everybody had almost given up on me. There was a certain move that Ivy made that she miscalculated and I just capitalized from that and won a game that lasted more than three hours." Phiona played eight games during the qualifying tournament and won them all.

When it came time for the national junior tournament in July, Katende again suggested that Phiona compete in the boys division to bolster her training for the upcoming Olympiad. Tournament organizers even changed the name of the boys division to "open" to accommodate Phiona.

Among the boys she defeated in the junior tournament were Richard Tugume and Benjamin Mukumbya. "I played Benjamin in the last match and played the way I do against a player who I am sure is strong and I just found myself winning the game," Phiona says. "It wasn't so much a surprise to me, but it was a surprise to Benja. I was so happy that day because I had won that division and no girl has ever done it in Uganda."

Phiona completed the tournament with six wins and one draw. The draw occurred against her younger brother Richard, who finished second overall in the open division.

"The tournament administrators were very shocked that Phiona had won," Katende says. "Many women showed up for the closing ceremonies because they had heard through the media about Phiona's performance. It was quite an exciting moment for many women in the country. Personally I gained some confidence that possibly Phiona could perform well in the Olympiad."

When she arrived in Istanbul in August, Phiona's attitude was different than it had been two years earlier in Khanty-Mansiysk. Says Phiona, "Unlike the first time at the Olympiad, I felt like I was somehow more positive this time because of the experience I had before in Russia and the confidence I had gained from the tournaments I had recently won."

Before Phiona's final Olympiad game, her record stood at two victories, three draws and three defeats. She was informed that if she won the next game she would earn a title. In her ninth game, on Sept. 7, 2012, Phiona defeated Azeb Menassie Zeleke of Ethiopia to become a Woman Candidate Master, the first step on the ladder toward Grandmaster. Phiona is the first woman from Uganda to ever obtain a title.

"I did feel some pressure before that last game started, but I played well through that pressure," Phiona says. "So when I won that game I was very happy because I had taken a big step forward in the game."

Shortly after arriving back in Uganda, Katende told Phiona that they would be traveling to America in December to help raise funds for Sports Outreach Institute. During a month-long visit, Phiona and Katende traveled to Washington, D.C., where they received a behind-the-scenes tour of the U.S. Capitol building through a friend of Rodney

Suddith. Their visit to the Marshall Chess Club in New York City, where Bobby Fischer often played, was written up as a "Talk of the Town" piece in *The New Yorker* magazine, and they went to Bristol, CT, where Phiona played chess on a giant board in the ESPN cafeteria against former New England Patriot Tedy Bruschi. They also visited many schools around the United States, including one that started a chess club inspired by Phiona's visit. Phiona says that her favorite memory from the trip was seeing the giant Christmas tree in Manhattan's Rockefeller Center.

"One thing I'm sure is that she's gained a very great deal of exposure which other people in the slums will never get to see in their lifetime," Katende says. "Unless you know what is out there, you will never work for the best, you will always settle for less. Now she has seen the world, she has seen things that it might take over a hundred years for our country to have, so having that picture in her mind is a great inspiration."

When Phiona returned to Uganda she shared photographs of her trip with her family and friends. Benjamin Mukumbya and Phiona's brother Brian both attend St. Mbuga with her on Popp scholarships. Phiona's younger brother Richard and Gloria Nansubuga plan to join them at St. Mbuga next year. Ivan Mutesasira studies at Busitema University and has represented his school during international chess tournaments. Phiona's older sister Night is still working at the Kibuye market. She has not been able to recover her kidnapped daughter, Rita.

Robert Katende has obtained a tract of land, the first step toward his dream of opening a Chess Academy and Children's Home for disenfranchised kids. In February of 2013, he and his wife had a second daughter. They named her Hope.

With funds she received from this book and a movie contract, Phiona's mother, Harriet, has moved out of Katwe into a house on the outskirts of Kampala where she can grow her own food and sell the surplus from her home. "That house is very good," Phiona says. "Even when I'm at school, now however much it rains, I don't have to worry about water getting in my mother's house, so I can now concentrate better at school. I know my mother is now fine, no worries about floods or even being evicted from the house, so that makes me very, very happy."

In April of 2013, Phiona was invited to return to the United States for the Women in the World Summit, where she was honored with a Women of Impact award. On the morning of April 4, the rooftop restaurant in New York City's Empire Hotel was closed for a game of chess. With the majestic skyline in the background, Phiona sat down at a chessboard. Across from her sat Garry Kasparov. The Ugandan junior champion and the former world champion competed for nearly two hours. "Playing Kasparov, I felt like it was not real to me because how can that be possible for someone who comes from Katwe?" Phiona says. "It was a game like in my dreams."

Kasparov won. So has Phiona.

Tim Crothers
July 2013

Tips from Phiona for Chess (and Life)

Believe in Yourself

You are meant to believe in yourself. If you are not sure of yourself, your best can't come out. When I first started playing chess, I didn't believe I could learn the game. Then I didn't believe I could become good. Then I didn't believe I could win a game. Then I didn't believe I could challenge a boy. But Coach gave me confidence and I won a game against a boy, and from that day I started to move forward more boldly and I began to believe in myself that I can win any game that I play. I have been amazed at what I could do in chess once I started believing in myself.

Challenge Yourself

It is easy to play against those opponents you know you can beat. But Coach has encouraged me to challenge myself and play as many games as I can against opponents who can beat me. When I go and play against someone who I believe is better than me, I know my chess will get better that day. I always learn something in a game when I am challenged.

Don't Get Too Excited

I don't ever get excited even when I'm in a winning position because I know that until the game is over I have to be really serious. One time I was playing in an Olympiad game and during preparations we had gone over various openings, so when I went to play I played a good opening and I managed to take a free piece and I realized my position was much better than my opponent's. I got so excited because I thought I was going to win. I ended up making a big blunder out of excitement and I lost a bishop. I eventually managed to win the game, but it was a serious struggle to come back. That day I learned that I can never get excited again until the game is over.

Don't Get Discouraged

I have played in so many games when I was in a bad position and I felt like resigning, but I always remember that Coach has given us advice about never resigning until the game is over. I hear those words in my head whenever my position seems hopeless and I just continue to endure and keep pushing myself. I have seen many examples that a chess game is never over, no matter how bad your position may be, until you are mated. You must continue to think. You must continue to plot. I have trained myself to believe that there is always a way out of trouble if I just continue thinking.

Be Patient

Once you have learned all the rules governing the pieces, it is time to learn to strategize and to plan. You are trying to create teamwork with your pieces. I encourage those I teach to be very patient in their planning. You cannot just win a game, you have to plan for it. I advise them not to always be in a hurry, but to first look at what the opponent has played and then try to read their mind. What are they planning? How can I stop that plan? Then how can I attack? How can I take control of the board? When I first started playing, I wanted to capture a piece on every move. One day I realized that you can win a chess game without capturing a single piece. That's when I realized that planning is more important than capturing. The best way to avoid blunders is to plan well. Every game is different. There are some games when I can never think more than one move ahead and there are others when I can plan beyond more than five moves ahead, but you must always be planning.

Have a Dream

The only way to become a good chess player is to work on your game every day, and I have found that it has helped me to have a dream. In my heart, I love chess and part of that is because I am working toward a goal. To be a big player in the game, I think you need to have a big dream, because if your dream is only to beat your brother or your father, then when you achieve that dream, you will quit because you have achieved that goal. My ultimate dream is to become a Grandmaster, and chasing that dream is what brings me back to the chessboard every day to try to become the first Grandmaster ever in my country.

Phiona Mutesi
Kampala, Uganda
July 2013

To buy any of our books and to find out
more about Abacus and Little, Brown, our authors
and titles, as well as events and book clubs,
visit our website

www.littlebrown.co.uk

and follow us on Twitter

@AbacusBooks
@LittleBrownUK

To order any Abacus titles p & p free in the UK,
please contact our mail order supplier on:

+ 44 (0)1832 737525

Customers not based in the UK should contact
the same number for appropriate postage
and packing costs.